To Sheryll,

The Dancer Returns

My favorite student. I live for your moans. You must learn to curb your enthusiasm!

In truth you are a dear, sweet friend and I am happy to have met you. Never change!

Love,
Susan Lee-Titus

The Dancer Returns

✦

From Victim to Victory

Susan Lee-Titus

iUniverse, Inc.

New York Lincoln Shanghai

The Dancer Returns
From Victim to Victory

iUniverse books may be ordered through booksellers or by contacting:

iUniverse
2021 Pine Lake Road, Suite 100
Lincoln, NE 68512
www.iuniverse.com
1-800-Authors (1-800-288-4677)

Because of the dynamic nature of the Internet, any Web addresses or links contained in this book may have changed since publication and may no longer be valid.

The views expressed in this work are solely those of the author and do not necessarily reflect the views of the publisher, and the publisher hereby disclaims any responsibility for them.

The prison presented in this book does not represent any one prison. The prison profiles mentioned in this book do not reflect any one person. Rather they are a combination of characters.

ISBN: 978-0-595-42414-6 (pbk)
ISBN: 978-0-595-91125-7 (cloth)
ISBN: 978-0-595-86750-9 (ebk)

Printed in the United States of America

WHAT OTHERS ARE SAYING ...

Susan's story is unforgettable, and from the first page, you'll be captivated. It is both honest and hopeful. Without the honesty, the hope would be unrealistic, and without the hope, the honesty would be devastating. Together, they provide a window into how God is with us at the worst moments of our lives, leading us from despair and victimhood to heroism and virtue. This beautiful book is for all of us, but especially for those who have suffered great trauma.

—Brian McLaren, author/activist. (brianmclaren.net)

In this brave and riveting book, Susan Lee-Titus takes us on a journey with a savage beginning but an amazing end. As the words unfold, the details of her devastating ordeal are shocking. Susan's account of her brutal attack and her painful recovery is heartbreaking. But out of Susan's brokenness emerges a triumphant woman whose life is focused on compassion toward other suffering people. This uplifting story will forever challenge what it means "to give back." I invite you to open your hearts and minds and experience the journey of *The Dancer Returns: From Victim to Victory*.

—Sterling Spell
Singer/Songwriter
with Northbound Band
www.Northbound-Rocks.com

I want to thank you,

Geri Rude

For your love, encouragement, treasured friendship, and prayers.
You will always be Sister Mary to me.

Ed Rude, a.k.a O'Rude

For your wisdom, patience, computer savvy, and caring spirit

Linda Hatcher

For your kindness, sweetness and helpful editing suggestions

To the Cedar Ridge Community

For constant support, encouragement, love, and prayers

In memory of my kind, beautiful friend and fellow dancer, Polly, who was brutally killed by her bipolar husband. You will dance forever in my heart as I imagine you dancing on heaven's ceiling.

Contents

Preface

Rape doesn't pick or choose by age, race, color, or creed; it is a matter of being at the wrong place at the wrong time. The brutal act of rape strikes, and for the victim, the memory strikes endlessly. Every two and a half minutes, somewhere in the United States, someone is sexually assaulted. Over half of these assaults go unreported. Statistics show that one out of every six American women will be a victim of sexual assault.[1] I want to put a face on those statistics: mine.

I was a successful, ambitious career woman, climbing the corporate ladder while pursuing my love of dance and aerobics. Life was perfect until the night that two men with sawed-off shotguns entered my dance class. Suddenly, nothing was the same and never would be again.

I wrote *The Dancer Returns: From Victim to Victory* especially for those who have suffered great trauma. But since no one leaves this world without encountering adversity, my book is for everyone. What makes my story different from many is the way I dealt with adversity by forgiving and reaching out to those in need.

On one level, my book is a story of both physical and mental recovery from a savage rape, but on another level, it is a painful odyssey from a self-centered, egotistical individual to a compassionate, caring teacher of formidable felons. The restoration in my life is illustrated by the fact that I am now able and willing to work directly with offenders as part of my prison outreach.

But healing didn't come easily. I suffered through all the stages of rape recovery. I was hospitalized with post-traumatic stress disorder (PTSD), an emotional and psychological reaction to trauma, which 70 percent of September 11 survivors experienced. Many soldiers returning from war battle PTSD with its paralyzing symptoms of fear, flashbacks, nightmares, insomnia, memory lapses, withdrawal, panic attacks, and other erratic behaviors. The consequences of PTSD—the physical suffering, the mental anguish, and the memories—can reverberate through a lifetime. At worst, it destroys lives; at best, it leaves severe scars with wounds that reopen from time to time. My book illustrates my fight with PTSD and how I conquered this crippling disease.

My story shows that it is not only possible to survive an atrocity but also to thrive and move forward to help and inspire others. Overcoming adversity is possible not only for victims of crime but for anyone who experiences loss, grief, trauma, battered women syndrome, sickness, severe accidents, relentless anger, or depression. My goal is to help people deal with the most debilitating and harsh realities of a cruel world.

However, before moving forward, a trauma victim must go through stages of grief and stages of recovery—a type of catharsis. These stages include shock, denial, fear, anger, depression, and then, hopefully, acceptance. My book illuminates each of these stages as I suffered through them.

Adversity changes a life forever. But change can take you in two directions—toward the dark or toward the light. Adversity introduced me to myself. I found out just how much courage, how much stamina, and how much endurance I really possessed. I discovered a new person and found a new perspective and a new purpose in life.

To weave the slender threads of a broken life into a firm pattern of meaning and responsibility is up to the victim. The will to live is fairly universal, but the way to make sense out of senseless suffering is individual. Every person must establish his or her own purpose in life. Some develop a new direction, turning to religion, charity, or a better appreciation of family and friends. Many realize that life is a gift and savor every moment.

Part of the work of moving on is to channel emotions and energy into activities that define, or even redefine, who we are. Successful survivors become fueled by a sense of mission to make the world a better place, to leave their imprint on some philanthropic work, or to give their lives significance. Others choose creative pursuits to express their passion for living. Many reach out and help the needy by volunteering, becoming a mentor, helping the homeless, or visiting nursing homes and hospitals.

In other words, reach out to someone who is in more pain than you are. You will find that pursuit to be the final step in healing.

… love rarely ever reaches out to save except it does it with a broken hand.

—Calvin Miller, in *The Singer*

1

Dancing in the Dark

5:50 PM

I sprinted in and lunged for the locker room, briefcase in one
hand, dance bag in the other. In rhythmic, almost choreographed movements, I peeled off my tailored, three-piece suit
and unraveled the pin-striped perfection of my corporate per-
sona. Sliding the pink leg warmers over my well-worn dance
shoes, I started to feel less like the new high-technology corporate trainer. My final act was to unpin my businesswoman's
bun. As ripples of long, wavy hair tumbled down, I bent slightly
and shook my head from side to side, banishing the business
world and inviting my artistic muse. I breathed deeply. I was
now in my element and could relax.

The stress of moving from the East to the West Coast was a
major adjustment: new job, new industry, new apartment, and
new state with a very different culture. I was still learning the
ropes at work, intent on success and climbing the proverbial
corporate ladder. Colleagues were colleagues, not friends. For
me, friendships were secondary. I wouldn't let them stand in
my way. I had major goals and an ambitious five-year plan. I
would be the youngest vice president in the industry at the close
of my fifth year.

My first goal was to hire a new assistant. The current girl had
totally messed up my slides for my first presentation, but luck-

ily, I had been one step ahead of her. And I was a huge hit. The executives actually stood and applauded. I smiled as I remembered their compliments. "Great job. Boston's loss is our gain." "I guess they grow them smart in Massachusetts. You are a major asset."

I loved the attention. It was what I'd always lived for: the sweet sound of applause. I was meant for applause and center stage. No doubt about that! *Shoot!* It was almost six o'clock. If I didn't hurry, I would lose my spot in front of the mirror! On to another thing I excelled at—dance.

6:45 PM

"Hold! Two, three, four. Don't you dare waiver. Five, six, seven. Release! Okay, take it down slowly. Now, up higher. Let's go for the burn!"

Ouch! I always lunge too deeply and pull something. But I will not stop. I will tough it out, work through the ache, and keep dancing. In fifteen more minutes, I would successfully complete a sixty-minute dance class *and* a ten-hour workday. I would grab the teacher after class. Maybe she would have a miracle cure. *No pain, no gain! That's what they say!*

7:00 PM

Whew! What a workout! I've got to get to the teacher before everyone crowds around her. Oh, too late. Why don't these foolish people get out of the way? I need to speak with her now. *This stinks!* I am second to the last in line. There is another injured dancer in back of me. What a waste of my precious time. The whole class has left except for Ruth, the teacher, Lauren, the other injured dancer and me.

I noticed two grubby men in their twenties with dark gray, hooded sweatshirts walk into the dance studio. "'Scuse us, any of you three ladies know where we can find a maintenance man around here?"

None of us answered.

"No? Thanks anyways."

"Those two give me the creeps. What are they doing here?" whispered Ruth. "I suggest we walk each other to our cars, mace in hand. Do you have mace, Susan?"

"No, I never needed it back home."

"Here, take my pocket knife just in case," Ruth said. The three of us left the studio. "Let's stay close and—"

"Down on the floor, or we'll blow your heads off! These are real, so don't make us use them. Give us your purses, now!"

He hit me on the back of my head with his gun. "You, blondie, turn over. What are you hiding in your hand? A knife? Joe, check the others for weapons. Were you planning to knife me? Give me that. I should use it on you. Cut up your face." He kicked me in the jaw with his heavy boot. "Get over there and take off your clothes!"

Oh my God, he's beating me. I'm going to be raped. Please, God, find help. If you loved me, you wouldn't let this happen to me. I don't deserve this. God, where are you?

"Hurry up, or I'll knock all your teeth out!"

God, he's pistol-whipping me, and I can't untie my shoes.... My tights won't come off.... Oh Lord, he smells awful like ... liquor ... like grease ... like dirt ... I'm gagging.... I'm hurting.... I'm bleeding.... My teeth are loose.... Now, he's raping me.... I'm going to die.... I want to die.... I can't stand it.... Let him shoot me, and it will be over.... He's stopping.... It's over.... Oh my

God, he's cutting the wires from the teacher's recorder. What will he do to me now?

"Turn over. Move it, or I'll use this gun. Lie face down. Put your hands behind your back. Hey, Joe, should we take her with us in the van?"

Please, God, you know I will be tortured if they kidnap me. Please let them kill me here. Give me the courage to make them shoot me. I cannot stand anymore abuse.

"No, she's not worth the trouble." He tied up Ruth and Lauren with the bandanas they wore as headbands."

Thank you, God.

"If any of you tell the police about this, you die. We know where you live."

Suddenly, eerie silence punctuated by staccato breathing and muffled sobs. Seconds contracted and dilated like wary eyes in shifting light amid the time-bending stillness. Then total, unnerving quiet—a cemetery quiet.

My God, if you let me live through this, I will try to find you again. I did love you once as a child, but somewhere along the way, I got too busy, too smart, and self-reliant. I thought that I didn't need you. I thought I knew it all. Imagine me with all my degrees and my successful career bound like a dog. But if I survive, I'll try to do some good in this world. I will reach out and help others less fortunate. I'll put others first. I'll use my talents to make a difference. If you let me live, I'll …

9:00 PM

"They've gone. It's over. I'll call the police." Ruth turned to Lauren. "You call and get an ambulance for Susan."

"I'll never be the same again."

"Yes, you will, honey. You will. I'll untie you." Ruth reached for the wires wrapped tightly around my crossed wrists and warped fingers.

"Are you crazy? Don't touch her. The police need to see her."

"I want my clothes. I want my green shorts."

"No, you can't wear them. They're evidence. The police need them."

"I want my little green shorts. They've stolen everything else. I want what's mine."

"Police! Nobody move. You first, miss. Give me your hands, and I'll untie you. Your finger looks broken." He took a handkerchief out of his pocket and wrapped it around my finger. "This will have to do until the paramedics arrive. What happened here?"

"We were robbed, and that blond girl, Susan, was raped. I'm her dance teacher. She needs me."

"Wait! Let us handle her," ordered one of the police officers. "You can't touch her until she's been examined. She can't wash. Her clothes need to be checked, too. Look at this mess. Purse items scattered all over the floor—combs, brushes, empty wallets. Those perps tore up this place."

A team of paramedics entered. "Who called for an ambulance?"

"Over here!" shouted the officer in charge. She's bleeding. She needs a doctor."

One of the paramedics knelt down. "Are you okay, miss? We'll get you to the hospital ASAP." He called to his partner. "Hurry, Bob, get the stretcher."

The paramedics helped me onto the stretcher and into the ambulance. The first one said, "Easy, easy. In you go. Bob, will you get her vitals?"

"Heart rate rapid," Bob reported, "pressure elevated, lip ripped and swollen, blood oozing from the mouth. What's that? I can't hear you, miss." I tried to speak, but found myself sputtering through blood and torn gums. "Say it again?" He jumped out of the ambulance.

"Hey, Bob!" the other paramedic shouted. "Why are you going back inside? What does she want?"

"She wants her teeth."

2

Prima in Pieces

10:00 PM, Hospital

"Seventeen years as a cop and I've never seen or heard anything like it. The teacher said they were all in a semicircle face down, hands tied behind their backs, blood everywhere. She was in the middle, quivering, her whole body a whimper. You know, she looks like the girl next door. I see her and I see my daughter, my sister, my wife. I feel for her. But then I file the report, and she just becomes another statistic. What can I do? I told her we'd catch those monsters no matter what it took. I promised her we would send a detective out right away. I gave my word. I wonder if she'll get over this completely. I mean, it has to change a person. How many recover? Are they ever really normal again?"

He has such a loud voice. Doesn't he know that I can hear everything he says? His face is crimson, and he's so big. Every time he questions me about it, he gets upset and breaks out in a sweat. He's so overweight I'm afraid he will have a heart attack. I'm not likely to have one. I have the benefit of dance and aerobics: an athlete's heart.

"This is the ER," said the first paramedic. "They will take real good care of you, Susan."

"Sorry, I couldn't get back in to look for your teeth," said the paramedic Bob. "The area was already cordoned off and considered a crime scene. They're looking for evidence, lifting finger-prints, stuff like that. At least you got the one tooth. Maybe it will bring you luck. Or better luck," he stammered.

The ambulance ride had been blurry—like I had dreamed it. The other two women had not really been hurt, so they had driven themselves to the hospital. I was alone with the two EMTs. I clutched the one tooth I had snatched from the floor.

When they wheeled me into the emergency room, we were met by a nurse. "Hello, I'm Nurse Higgins," the woman said, "head nurse of this wing of the hospital."

She escorted us to a back room, and then the EMTs rolled me gently onto the bed. A model of efficiency, Nurse Higgins drew the curtain around my bed and addressed the two men. "I'll take it from here, gentlemen. Do you have her paperwork? I see her vitals; that's all I need." She spoke to me in a consoling tone, "I'll give you something to make you feel better after I check your vital signs. Are you allergic to any medication? No? Well, that's positive."

The police officer poked his head through the drawn curtain. "We still need to ask her questions. Do you think we can talk with her after you're finished?"

"Yes. But give the medication time to work, she is very anxious." She pulled the curtain tighter around my bed area and looked at me, saying, "I'm giving you more than I normally would to someone your size because your heart rate and blood pressure are through the roof. But you can help by breathing deeply. Now breathe for me, Susan, nice, slow breaths." She then backed out slowly, eyes fixed on me and my deep breaths. "Make it brief, Officer," Nurse Higgins ordered.

One green pill, one orange, and one shot in the arm—that's what the nurse gave me. She claims for someone my size, it should calm me down? Not a chance. I will never be calm again. I can't stop shaking. She promises the doctor will be in soon, and then she leaves me alone with this cop.

He chooses his words carefully. He is trying to be gentle, sensitive. He looks at me intently, like he is watching the end of a ballet and waiting for the curtain to come down.

So this is what it feels like to be a rape victim. This is how people react to you … how they look at you … how they treat you. Like a fragile prima ballerina … a prima in pieces.

"The hour I first believed." Lines from the hymn "Amazing Grace" keep floating through my head; it's one of the few religious songs I know. "Amazing grace, how sweet the sound that saved a wretch like me! I once was lost but now am found, was blind but now I see." I read somewhere that it was Elvis Presley's favorite.

Elvis … hymns … the plump cop … Maybe I've gone insane, or maybe I just can't stand to think about what's happened.

Where is the doctor? They make you wait so long.

Cutting a swath through the cops and medical attendants came young, buxom Nurse Ferris. Her flame-haired, fluffy curls flounced as she sashayed toward my bed. Her flashy ankle bracelet caught the corner of my sheet.

"I need your insurance card," she demanded. Her full-on stare made my stomach spasm. Even though I averted my eyes, I could feel hers rudely scrutinizing me as if she had never seen a rape victim.

"I was robbed," I explained. "They stole my purse and my wallet with my insurance card inside." This time, I stared at her, noticing that under the fluorescent lights, her freckles looked like a gallery of stars.

"Well, then, give me your Social Security number," she insisted with forced normality.

I complied.

"Okay, are you pregnant?"

"No," I snapped.

"Do you take recreational drugs?" probed the nurse.

"Me? No. I'm not the criminal." *I'll need even more medication after dealing with this insensitive broad.*

"Nurse, I think she's had enough for now," said the police officer. "I think we all should leave and let her rest. We'll send a detective out to your house, and he can finish the questioning. Good night, miss."

God, I need you. I'm alive! I survived! But I'm broken in a million pieces. I'm scared. I don't know what to do. I'm alone here on the West Coast. I only know a few people from work.

"Nurse Higgins, bring me a rape kit for the forensic exam," ordered a stocky, curly-haired doctor as he swaggered into the room. "I'm Dr. Alan Levine. I'll use the standard rape kit to get the samples we need; then I'll examine you for any other problems."

It hurts. He is too rough, too methodical. He lacks gentle hands, a gentle spirit. The nurse opens a large paper bag, and he drops the samples inside. She seals the bag, labels it, and walks away. It's as if little pieces of you are handed off to strangers, never to be seen again and never to be a part of your body.

I wondered how many paper bags there were in the hospital and the police station. Inside each paper bag was a story waiting to be told, and inside, was a crime waiting to be solved.

"You're pretty badly beaten," commented the doctor, "but no broken bones. No broken cheekbones. Your finger is just sprained probably from the way they tied you up. Keep the splint on for at least three days, longer if the throbbing continues. The bruises and cuts will heal. You'll just need to have most of your teeth replaced; you'll want to see a dentist soon. I'll give you a prescription to prevent infection. That's it. You can go home now," Levine concluded.

"But Doctor, I'm afraid to drive home. I'm not from around here. I'm from Boston. I have no license, no money, and no purse. They stole everything. Can't I stay overnight? I can call someone from work in the morning."

"Sorry, miss, we have no available beds," the doctor stated. "The nurse will clean you up and then bring you a phone. You can stay here until someone comes for you. But then you'll have to go."

I bet no one ever gave you a prize for bedside manner. My mind raced, thinking of whom I could call this late. Carole—she lived near me, and she seemed like a caring person. When I reached her, she said that she and her husband would come right away.

All that medication never kicked in; I still couldn't stop shaking and crying. It didn't help that I was all alone in a sparse, cold, clinical room behind a closed metal door. It was as if the hospital considered a rape victim an infectious pariah and wanted to protect other patients from the social outcast. Rape wasn't catching, not physically, anyway. But like the lepers of old, people didn't want to be around you.

Well, I had just been through a near-death experience and had met the good, the bad, and the ugly. The good were the EMTs, Nurse Higgins, and the police. The bad were my assailants; the ugly were callous Nurse Ferris, and the cocky doctor. I suspected they were linked romantically; certainly, they were two of a kind with their glacial personalities.

I wondered when Carole would get here. There was nothing to do but think; I needed to force myself to think about what had happened so I could figure out what I should do next. My heart began a slow, steady thud.

I'm a rape victim. From this moment until the day I die, I will be branded a rape victim. How will I ever get through this? How does anyone get through it? Was the cop onto something when he suggested that it has to change a person? Will I ever be normal again? I know I will never forget that marrow-deep terror.

I soon found out that my ordeal was just beginning. Next came the challenge of living the rest of my life as a member of an exclusive club. The club dues are high and the initiation painful, but the membership is for life. The roster includes groups of people admitted solely because of nationality; some get in because of religious beliefs while others make it because of skin color. Some are just in the wrong place at the wrong time and become pawns in the politics of terrorism; some are used as tools of war. Some are newborns, christened with the surname "crack baby." Individuals, too, can become members. Why, one woman was simply a lone jogger in Central Park!

The price of admission to this club? You must be a victim.

Victim. Webster defines it as any sufferer from a destructive, injurious, or adverse action or agency—a person or animal sacrificed or regarded as a sacrifice. The term can apply to an individual, or it can encompass an entire group, as with the Holocaust. Rape victims make up a very exclusive club. One out of six women will be raped sometime during her life. And of those women, the prognosis for recovery is not promising. Some women have committed suicide as late as two years after a rape experience.

I discovered that the doctor's curt response to me was indicative of the world's response to victims. No one wants you around because you remind them that bad things can happen to innocent people in ordinary circumstances. What could be more ordinary than an aerobic-dance class at six in the evening? I wasn't at fault. I couldn't have done anything to prevent it. And that is what scares them—happenstance—a flash of fate, the frightening possibility that life can change in an instant. No one wants to believe rape can happen to them, and the sight of a rape victim reminds them that it can. So they try to avoid you.

Carole and her husband not only picked me up at the hospital, they insisted that I stay overnight at their house. Though I didn't sleep well, I felt safer with others around. Plus, Carole told me she would tell my boss what had happened so I could stay at home and call him when I was ready.

The moment I got home, I took a long, very hot shower, and I scrubbed and scrubbed with a rough loofah until my skin was raw red. I had to get his smell off of me; I had to wipe away the rape, wipe away the night. I wanted to feel clean and pure again. And as I washed with a vengeance, I was reliving the moments of the rape, minute by breathless minute.

When I finished my shower, I felt extremely sore, and my body looked sunburned. But I felt that I had taken the first small step toward physical recovery.

True to their word, the day after the rape, the Los Angeles Police Department phoned to confirm that they had assigned a detective to my case. He would stop by to see me.

Victimization is not limited to those who have been on the receiving end of crime. In today's violent times, many police officers are victims of stress-related illnesses. My detective suffered from an ulcer. He had just finished an investigation of child abuse when he was assigned to me. He told me he promised himself for the sake of his ulcer that he would never again get personally involved in a case. However, as he explained it, "I figured this would be easy: some stuck-up broad from Boston. But then I opened the door, and there you were, all red-eyed and shaking. And I thought, *there goes my ulcer.*"

He was a kind and decent man, dedicated to his work, yet counting the days to retirement. When he arrived the following day to take me to the police artist, he brought me a little teddy bear. He said, "Now, maybe your experience will be *bearable.*" He loved puns and did his best to make me smile.

The detective left me alone with the police artist for a while. The artist had to be patient and sensitive because I was afraid to describe my assailants. After all, they had threatened me, and I had taken them very seriously. Also, I had only gotten a good look at one of them when he had come through the door, pointing his gun. "Keep your eyes closed, or you're dead," he had repeated during the rape, and I had squeezed my eyes so tightly that they had burned. My eyelids had ached for two days afterward.

As the artist kindly prodded me, I began to remember. I said, "The eyes—those glassy, penetrating eyes—pupils dilated and fixed on the targets. They burned brightly like a deranged, diabolical Adolf Hitler or Charles Manson. I'll never forget those eyes." The artist sketched rapidly as I talked. "The guy had a gravelly, hoarse voice that was frightening."

"Take a look at this," the artist said. "Did I sketch the eyes the way you remember them?"

"Yes, but the face was longer and thinner; the nose was longer, too."

He sketched some more. "Is this better?"

"Yes, that's him," I whimpered and hung my head in despair. Gently, he put his forefinger under my chin and lifted my face. Smiling, he brushed my hair back. "You have a widow's peak. It is a sign of beauty. You shouldn't hide it."

"I don't like to think about those things anymore," I said. "They just get you raped."

"Hush," the artist said, "you mustn't blame yourself. You are a lady, and the closest those criminals will ever come to one. Rape is a crime of power over someone more vulnerable. They had guns; you were vulnerable. I know it's hard to appreciate anything, especially a widow's peak, right now, but you will get over this. Time heals."

My detective came back with a box from the local bakery. "Anyone interested in doughnuts?" he asked. He put the box in front of me.

I almost gagged. "I can't. I can't swallow."

"Sure you can," he urged.

"No, ever since it happened, I can't swallow."

Both the police artist and my detective looked appalled. Reluctantly, my detective handed the box to another cop, who thanked him profusely.

My detective tried in every way to make my life more pleasant. As much as I liked him and appreciated him, he also introduced me to a side of police work that gave me nightmares—lineups. Lineups were nothing like I had seen on television where one person would view a line of alleged criminals. Instead, a group of victims would be shuffled from one room to another. Then, huddled together in an overcrowded auditorium, the victims would watch as criminals, behind glass, were marched out on stage like movie stars.

My fellow victims seemed like a sea of suffering—dozens of dazed, defeated, silent people with stone faces, symbols of muted agony, eyes darting, suspicious of everyone. Some clutched purses to their chests as if protecting an infant. One man repeatedly grasped his wallet and counted the contents. An older woman nervously removed the spotless, white gloves from her hands, revealing a missing finger on her left hand. In a robbery attempt, she was ordered to surrender a ring. Years of marriage and a few extra pounds rendered the ring stuck for life. The robber cut her finger off.

And then there were the survivors' stories: *Monday Night Football* on a balmy California night. The front door was open to let in the breeze. Father and son were watching the game. Mom and two neighborhood women were styling each other's hair. Suddenly, six men with sawed-off shotguns walked right through the front door, tied up father and son, then raped each of the women. Father and son looked on helplessly.

I heard tales of the epitome of man's inhumanity to man: At a Los Angeles street corner, a woman got out of her car to call home to check on her infant son. Five men grabbed her, raped her, tortured her, and then took her keys and ran over her with her own car. That woman survived. Many don't. So those of us who do feel compelled to tell their stories as well as our stories. It is our responsibility—the responsibility of memory.

The maimed. The tortured. The crime victims. They were pawns in the hands of criminals who fulfilled themselves through cruelty. And I was one of these broken people. I cried at every lineup. I became withdrawn, almost mute, a startling contrast to my normal, very verbal, extroverted personality.

One time when I cried during the lineup, my detective cautioned me, "If you see the rapist, don't show any emotion because they will say you are prejudicing the others. The rapist probably harmed other people here."

I answered, "I don't see him. It's just that everyone up there is so ugly, it scares me."

"Well, I'll try to have them arrested for showing an obscene face in public," he responded.

Humor in the face of adversity. My detective tried all kinds of things to make the weekly lineup experience a little less frightening. Nothing worked.

It also didn't help when he arrived at my office one day, interrupted the training session I was conducting, and said that I needed to go somewhere with him. He wouldn't reveal where we were headed. We ended up at the police station. I was anxious, but I followed him into a small, sealed, nondescript room with an inky smell. "We've been waiting for you," snapped the officer behind the desk.

When I frowned, my detective pulled me aside and said, "We lifted three sets of fingerprints off the floor where you were lying face down. We figure if we get your fingerprints, we can eliminate one set."

The officer behind the desk thrust his fingerprint pad in front of me. I wept through the entire process. *I'm innocent; yet, I'm in a police station being fingerprinted like a common criminal.* It was all too overwhelming.

"Well, I don't know if we'll catch your assailants, but if you ever commit a crime anywhere in the United States, we have your fingerprints on file, and we can nab you in a nanosecond," joked my detective.

But humor was lost on me. I just wanted to wake up from this nightmare. I was deteriorating; my life was ruptured; my body was tired; my heart was frozen.

I developed a constant tremor in my right hand. In front of other people, I would only drink coffee from a Styrofoam cup because the rattling of china attracted so much attention. Sleeping and eating were impossible. I was like a frightened animal lost in the woods, not knowing which path to follow because all seemed foreboding and treacherous.

I was too terrified to put out my own trash, let alone venture out to the grocery store. Constantly cowering in fear, I was afraid of strangers, afraid of the dark, and most afraid that it might happen again.

A co-worker referred me to a psychiatrist, and I began the painful journey of trying to understand what had transpired.

I was apprehensive about my first meeting. I walked into an ordinary brick building and trudged up to the second floor where the office was located. I entered a tiny waiting area. A small aquarium was the main focal point. I parked myself in front of it, eschewing the usual magazine offerings. A door opened, and a tall man with a lion's mane of snow white hair and warm blue eyes smiled and directed me into his office.

His eyes welled up when I told my story. He didn't respond for a few minutes, which felt like an eternity. This was my first time in a psychiatrist's office, so I didn't have any expectations. Finally, he spoke. "When individuals come and relate their problems, I might diagnose them as paranoid or neurotic. But what happened to you was real. Your fear, insomnia, and appetite loss are understandable. Getting over this won't be easy."

I said, "I also have a fever but no other symptoms, like, a cold or a sore throat. So I don't understand what is happening to me physically."

"Your immune system has been compromised," the psychiatrist said. "Severe stress and trauma can do that quite easily. There is a mind-body connection. You might need to be hospitalized at some point."

"I'd prefer to try aspirin and orange juice," I offered.

"My best advice?" the psychiatrist suggested. "Try not to keep your feelings inside. If you are angry, pound the walls. Scream. I believe in primal scream therapy; cry till you feel you are all cried out. What happened to you was an atrocity, and if you keep those feelings bottled up, you will never recover. Tell me, what do you fear most?"

"That it will happen again," I said. "Can you promise me that I'll never be raped again?"

"No, no one can promise that."

"I thought that's what you'd say. So I'm preparing myself. Every night, I go through this ritual. I walk into my bathroom and stand in front of the mirror and stare. Then I flash back to the night of the rape, how scared I was, how much it hurt. But I know that the next time, it will be worse. So I force myself to picture the rapist pulling out a knife and slashing my face. I make myself feel the pain, the terror, the devastation of a ruined face. If I prepare myself, then when it really happens, maybe it won't hurt so much. Maybe I won't be as scared as I was the first time ... maybe ... maybe."

3

Break Dance

"**S**usan called me that night," Carole said to a co-worker. "I went to the hospital to pick her up. I saw the other two. No doubt in my mind why she was chosen. She was the prettiest one, and she has that gorgeous, long hair. That's why they picked her to rape. I'm sure of it. Come on, your makeup looks fine. Our break is over. I have to get back to my desk."

Four weeks after the rape, there I sat, long hair and all, behind the door of a stall in the ladies' room. I felt like a victim once again—a victim of bored co-workers, hungry for sensational tidbits to add spice to an otherwise routine day. The voices of gossip had spouted various opinions on what had sired this calamity in my life. Today, it was my hair.

I left the ladies' room, my neck tense with the daily effort of holding my head high. Till five o'clock every day, I tried to keep up the charade of a miraculous recovery—emotions intact. I worked hard to show I was ready to resume my life and pick up where I had left off, to act as if nothing had happened, to assume the pretense of being normal. To the world, I appeared to be a "together" woman when, in reality, all that was left were shards of a smashed self.

Daily, I treaded a high, thin wire, mindful of the abyss below. It was an exhausting balancing act between sanity and insanity—between the real world and the subtext in my mind. Voices … voices within … voices ran constantly through my head, never giving me a moment's peace. I heard many voices: the voices of the gossips, the police, concerned friends. And his—the rapist's—the loudest voice that echoed incessantly, punctuating my every activity. While brushing my teeth, washing dishes, standing at the water cooler, driving my car, I heard it: "You get over there and take off your clothes." I couldn't get rid of that voice.

Driving home from work each night with clenched teeth, tightly gripping the steering wheel, emotions ready to spill, I barely made the ten-minute ride. I parked directly in front of my apartment building but looked in every direction before getting out of my car.

Though it was a secure building, I scanned the empty hallway before entering. In front of the door to my apartment, I checked the peep to make sure that no one was waiting inside. I slipped through the doorway, quickly slamming the door. I flipped the deadbolt and then hooked the safety chain. I retrieved a kitchen chair and pushed it up against the door. This was my nightly ritual.

Finally, safe inside, my tiny apartment became the framework of a surrealistic painting where hazy, phantasmagoric figures escaped from their frame into my living room. Nightly, they gave an enervating performance that ranged from ranting and raving to weeping and whimpering. I didn't need my psychiatrist to tell me these allegorical figures in my mind were my wide range of emotions played out in the secure confines of my home. The figures also mirrored my current demeanor, as irregular as a Picasso painting.

My eight-hour office portrayal of tightly sealed emotions and total control gave way to abandon—one final primal scream that seemingly was my best defense against madness. Totally spent, I crawled into bed to catch one or two hours of fitful rest, but not sleep—sleep meant uncontrollable nightmares.

Lying awake and staring at the ceiling, dappled with the shadows of the street light, I heard strange, suspicious sounds and imagined prowlers. I compulsively checked and rechecked locked doors and windows once, twice, three times till the chirping of birds and the light of early dawn heralded the haven of morning. Then, barely functioning, I again donned my corporate garb to re-create my role as "the businesswoman."

Before I left my apartment each day, I went through a morning ritual. I fanatically hid anything of value; I was convinced that I would be robbed again. Tearing off squares of tin foil, I wrapped up all my credit cards and put them in the refrigerator. *With my luck*, I thought cynically, *I'll get a hungry burglar who thinks the silver wrappings contain food.*

Driving home from work this particular Friday night, something else was bothering me. *She has that gorgeous, long hair.* I couldn't get that comment out of my mind. Was that why they had picked me? Was I to blame? Did my hair attract attention? Never again did I want to be noticed. I just wanted to blend in with the crowd. I didn't want to be chosen.

Frantically, I opened the three locks on my front door and performed my nightly ritual. I knew what I had to do. I went straight to my sewing box and then hurried into the bathroom. With trembling but determined hands, I cut off the silky strands that had once been my pride and joy, that had saucily bounced to dance tunes, that had kept me warm during New England winters, and that represented youth, vitality, and, above all, femininity. Soon, my hair was almost all gone, and I didn't care. I didn't want to be pretty. I just wanted to be safe.

Breathless, perspiring, and slightly delirious, I looked from the hair-strewn floor to the mirror. I had scalped myself and had left jagged, uneven wisps in place of golden locks. Coming to my senses, I vowed to visit a hairdresser the next day.

To many women, hairdressers are like bartenders—true confessors, psychiatrists, best friends, counselors. Realizing that my new hairdo was not the result of a talent for precision cutting, my stylist gently inquired. Needing someone to talk to, I told him the whole story. He responded, "God doesn't want you to make yourself unattractive. What happened wasn't your fault. Bad things happen to good people. You will recover. I know you can't believe that now, but you'll see."

Patched up, primped, and polished with a shorter but professional-looking coif, I thought that, at least, I looked normal. I emerged from the salon an hour later. My hairdresser, sensitive to the fact that I was still apprehensive about walking alone even in early afternoon, graciously escorted me to my car. Then he did a remarkable thing; he got into my car and prayed with me.

Despite such acts of kindness, I still was very anxious. I found it difficult, if not impossible, to swallow. I existed on liquids alone. Peggy, a nice woman from work, offered me her home. She was recently divorced with two small children. I had requested a transfer back to Massachusetts, so the situation would be temporary. She thought that living with a family might relieve my fear.

The same week I moved in, Peggy's house was robbed while we were at work. I became hysterical. Wherever I went, criminals seemed to find me. I felt like a hunted animal. I didn't feel safe anywhere. I trembled uncontrollably. My mind felt blurry, foggy. I heard my heart thumping, and I heard those ceaseless voices. I felt like I was losing my mind.

I needed to talk to someone from home—someone to reassure me. In the aftermath of rape, one of the hardest things to deal with is friends and family who respond inadequately when the victim is in desperate need. On the day Peggy's house was robbed, I made one phone call; it was a sole attempt to save my sanity. "Peggy's house has just been robbed, and I need to talk with someone from home. I feel like I'm losing my mind."

"Well, what do you expect me to do three thousand miles away? Go find some doctor to give you a pill. I was taking a nap, and you woke me up. Now, don't bother me with things I can't do anything about."

Click went the phone, and snap went my mind. I felt something sever, something break inside. Then, in a jumble of actions and feelings, many things happened simultaneously. I heard a buzzing, as if a cluster of bees was surrounding me. I experienced an unexplainable inner sensation like an electric shock, combined with a vibration similar to a metal spring being coiled and uncoiled. I was like a machine that went awry. It seemed as if I was in another dimension—eerie, misty, foggy. And even worse than this haze was the sensation of losing all power, a terrifying seepage of strength and sanity. My breath was ragged, uneven. My arms and legs were limp. I felt like a rag doll. My heart clenched into a fist of quiet pain.

I had an appointment that day with my psychiatrist. Somehow, I made it to his office. I told him about the day's events from the robbery to the phone call to the feeling that my mind had snapped. He had spoken to me before about entering a hospital. I thought the purpose was to get my appetite and sleeping patterns back.

Now, he told me gently, "Susan, I really think that you need to be hospitalized and not just for the physical reasons. You see, they're symptomatic of the turmoil in your mind."

"Oh my God, you're talking about a mental institution!" I jumped out of my chair as if I had received an electric shock. I paced frantically, fighting the tears that threatened to flow.

"Well, yes, a hospital such as that." He remained frozen in his chair, his eyes following my frenzied footwork.

I opened the door to the empty waiting room, stomping over to the aquarium and whacking its wooden top. I felt the tiny fish were the only living creatures more vulnerable than I was, and even they had glass and wood protection. I pounded the top once more, and my doctor winced. "I'm not crazy," I said. "I just had something terrible happen to me. Can't you understand that?"

"Yes, I can," said my psychiatrist. "And you're not crazy. You're suffering from something known as post-traumatic stress disorder, an emotional and psychological reaction to the trauma that you have gone through. It is a delayed reaction to the rape. The mind, to protect itself, initially shuts down and denies the event. But your subconscious doesn't forget, and it eats away at you till you face it. Denial is one of the stages of rape recovery, and you are in that stage now. The first phase is shock, what you described as being paralyzed with fear—a zombie-like state where you are frozen, afraid to move or feel. Not surprisingly, actual fear is the next phase, and it includes the shakes, the relentless voice of the rapist, and the flashbacks to that night. I think you are still in that stage, as well."

"What others stages do I have to look forward to?"

"Well, for most rape survivors, the next stage is anger, followed by depression, and then, hopefully, acceptance," said my psychiatrist. "I've given you a thumbnail sketch, but we will discuss each one in depth as you experience them."

My temples throbbed, and I kept hitting my forehead with the back of my hand to stop the sound of blood thundering through my head. "But entering a mental hospital will just scare me and make me worse."

"You have a stereotype in your mind," said my psychiatrist. "The hospital I'm thinking of is a beautiful place. There is only one caveat. Admission to this hospital will stay on your record for life, and anyone who investigates your past can find it out. If you remain in a normal profession, this fact shouldn't hurt you. If you choose a more visible career, say, something like politics, an issue could be made. But I think it's a risk worth taking."

"What if I refuse to go?" I asked.

"You can refuse," he said. "Only you can sign yourself in, but if you refuse, you may never recover, and then someone will have to commit you, maybe for life. You've had a partial breakdown. Don't wait till you've broken down completely."

4

The Dancer Returns

Two days after my psychiatrist recommended a hospital, I drove myself to a secluded area with lots of trees and flowers. The place was in vast contrast to the clinical, antiseptic, sterile environment I expected. I was greeted at the door by a pleasant, matronly receptionist who admitted me. She then reached under her desk and touched something. Two female medical personnel arrived and escorted me into a room with a single table.

So far, the experience seemed painless. And then it happened. The attendants stood on either side of me. One took my coat and sweater; the other took my purse and emptied the contents on the flat table. Quickly and nimbly, she sifted through my things while the other investigated the pockets of my coat and sweater. They looked surprised when I began to tremble.

Don't they know that's what the rapist did to my purse and all my belongings? Don't they know that they are re-creating the night of the rape? Don't they know it's like being raped again?

The spoils of their pillaging included a nail file, nail polish remover, comb, aspirin, head bands, barrettes, and rubber bands. The collection they appropriated, trying to explain that other patients might try to harm themselves with these items.

And then the ultimate degradation. I had to remove my clothing in front of them to make sure I wasn't harboring any drugs or weapons of any kind. I was humiliated. As I started to untie my shoes and remove my socks, I remembered a page I had read that morning from the devotional *Each New Day* by Corrie ten Boom, the Dutch concentration-camp survivor, convicted for hiding Jews in her home during the war. I tried to recall what Corrie wrote.

> In the concentration camp we went through the ordeal of being stripped of all our clothing and made to stand for several hours. It was more difficult than anything else we experienced.[1]

I was now stripped of everything—pride, possessions, identity, respect. To these hospital personnel, I was just another troubled person—no one special. I had suffered rape and brokenness, and now, I was in a mental institution. What could be worse? I came here so that I wouldn't break down completely as my doctor warned. Now, it seemed like I had made a horrible decision.

A routine physical followed the humiliating search. My vital signs were taken, and I was weighed and measured. I was to be weighed daily because weight fluctuations could signal depression and thus extend the hospital stay. That realization was shocking enough to bring back my appetite. Appropriately enough, the first place they took me was to the cafeteria for an early dinner.

In sharp contrast to my perception of a drab mental hospital, I saw a dining room replete with every primary shade on the color wheel. It was as if a psychiatrist-turned-artist had dipped his brush into a palette of optimism and, in broad strokes, had painted a picture of humanity as he wished it to be. Such an artist could control the hue of the decor but not the unmistakable doomsday aura of the patients.

Damaged people with faces of despair and submission shuffled in to repeat the reluctant ritual of a hospital meal. Looking from one to the other, I wondered what brought them here. Were they also victims of crime? Had they been abused? What cruel blow had life dealt them?

"She just had shock treatment," my assigned dining mate said, lowering her voice as if revealing a whispered curse. "All of them had the treatments," she said, pointing to a corner dining table.

I saw a mass of organisms with a human shape attired in cadaverous gray hospital garb, a symbol of their almost extinguished humanity. They stood out from the rest of us, who were allowed to wear jeans. Their faces were like ghost towns. Something else was different too—their eyes—they were dead. The whole table looked like a den of death, emitting a whiff of the grave.

My table was different. Energy abounded. Nervous tapping and clanking of silverware were the norm. Another new arrival, whose boyfriend was staying through the meal, joined our group. He explained that his girlfriend was bulimic, and even though she seemed painfully thin and barely touched her food, he said that she might come down at night and devour the contents of the entire kitchen—then go back to her room and "purge."

My roommate was pregnant for the fourth time. She had previously lost all three babies for unknown physical reasons. She seemed fine physically, so her doctor thought the problem might be psychological. To safeguard this pregnancy, her family had hospitalized her.

I thought about all these people as I lay in bed that night, trying to sleep. What did they do to deserve this? What did I do to deserve this? If God was everywhere, was he in here, too? Or did he make it a habit to stay out of mental institutions?

Lord, do you hear me? What is the purpose of all this? Will it make me a better person? Are you trying to teach me something—humility, sensitivity? In the troubled eyes of these patients, can I still see you?

I tossed and turned, unable to relax. Then I heard it, faintly at first and then louder and more persistent: shuffling, slow but steady. The nightly shuffle in the corridor of the crazed came alive. Broken spirits assembled, with faces etched in grief, bodies too anxious to sleep. It was the corridor where many lives crossed paths. From CEOs to truck drivers, no one was exempt from mental illness, and these restless souls exhibited their problems by roaming the halls. The staff referred to the odd parade as the "nighttime blues."

By 1:00 in the morning, the parade ended as attendants rounded up these wanderers and herded them back to their rooms. They started with the main corridor and then proceeded into the bowels of the hospital, searching for wayward phantoms. Any recalcitrant ramblers would be constrained by medication, restraints, and as a last resort, lockup.

I listened to doors opening and closing until I heard the clang of the last lock, a steely reminder of where I was—a mental institution.

In addition to the weirdness of the night, I also wasn't prepared for what would happen the next day—a group-therapy session. Supposedly, this format helped people open up and see that they shared common problems. But it didn't seem to me that they had grouped people very well. They put me in a group of women who had all attempted suicide. *Suicide.* The word shocks and silences. And so it did to this sullen group until one very large, very heavy black woman looked at me and asked in a hissing tone, "What are you in here for? What problem could you have with your pretty little face and your pretty little body?"

I froze. I couldn't move. I couldn't speak. I was terrified. Everyone seemed to be waiting for my response, including the counselor. All my life, I'd been "mouthy." Words were my business. I used them to persuade and to cajole—mainly, to get whatever I wanted. I used my communication skills to get out of traffic violations, to get jobs, raises, and bargains. I always stood up for my rights. No one pushed me around.

Now, I cowered before this woman. I shook visibly. I just wanted to get out of there. The counselor moved on to other people, but this woman glowered at me the entire hour as if I represented something she hated.

My next appointment was alone with my psychiatrist, who had referred me to this hospital. When I related this harrowing encounter, he confronted me with a reality that I had not yet dealt with. "Susan, have you considered that maybe you froze because this woman was black as were your assailants? Don't forget, they assaulted you verbally, too. There is nothing shameful or racist about being afraid. You need to face this reality before you can heal."

He also explained that the woman's reason for attacking me was that in my appearance and my demeanor, I represented the establishment. She probably felt that her economic plight and less-than-adequate lifestyle were due to an unfair society—which, to her, I symbolized.

For me, this hospitalization was my humbling. I had always prided myself on intellectual achievements and talents. I was a straight-A student and a magna cum laude graduate. And I thought that I was better than most people, especially the kind of people hospitalized here. I figured their problems were due to weakness, their lack of employment to laziness, and their emotional breakdowns to genetic, inherited deficiencies.

And now, I was one of them—a patient in an institution that questioned my sanity. In Victorian times, they would have called it an asylum. My pride, which propelled me to achieve and excel, was smashed. My arrogance was totally gone.

Never again would I think that I was superior to others. Never again could I hear the cackling of panhandlers or see the incessant twitching of a bag lady, the trembling hands of an alcoholic, the begging of street children, the writhing of the addicted, or the frozen resignation of the homeless without feeling compassion. Never again could I see and hear these things and look down my arrogant nose. Because now I was one of them.

My psychiatrist concluded our visit with a statement for me to think about. "The makers of oriental rugs deliberately weave a single flaw into their complex patterns because perfection is a divine, not a human, prerogative. Welcome to the world of the flawed, Susan!"

It was true. I had been driven to perfection in every area of my life. I was the quintessential member of the "me" generation lost in visions of perfection, of being forever healthy, young, beautiful, and strong. And in this fanatical pursuit, I never saw the need for compassion and sensitivity. Those virtues just got in my way.

There was nothing wrong with a healthy self-esteem and with taking care of oneself in a difficult world. But I had been self-absorbed, catering to *only* myself. Now, I began to realize that it was important to recognize, respect and help all human beings.

That night, I was able to think of my therapy group as human beings—not disturbed, violent animals driven to suicide to put themselves out of their own misery. Something had driven them to this point, suggested my new, compassionate nature. "There but for the grace of God go I" was the adage that came to mind.

I still didn't know how to handle that woman in group therapy. Agitated, I punched my pillow and tugged at my blankets. My mind raced, and my thoughts collided, and then suddenly, I bolted out of bed. I remembered her—the girl in the pink dress. That ten-year-old girl with the pretty, pink dress with matching pink ribbons loomed large and lovingly in my memory.

My aunt taught the fifth grade and invited me, her five-year-old niece, to visit her classroom for a day. I brought my lunch and felt like a very big girl. During recess, my aunt asked a group of girls to baby-sit me. Included was the girl in the pink dress, who said, "Let's teach her to jump rope." Very patiently and kindly, she taught me and encouraged me. "Come on, you can do it. Look at her. She's so little, but she can do it."

By the time I got to the first grade, I was the jump-rope queen. To this day, I have a warm and grateful feeling for that girl in the pink dress. I'm not sure if it registered with me at five, but that young girl was black. It is true that you have to be taught to hate. Hate wasn't present in that schoolyard that day. And I vowed it would not be present in my recovery, including hatred toward the woman in my group therapy.

Bracing myself for another tense day, I entered the group-therapy room, taking my seat beside the counselor for protection. It was one minute to nine, and that woman hadn't appeared, yet. Maybe I was safe. Through the back door, however, she waddled in and plopped right down beside me. Before the counselor could begin, the woman put her face close to mine like a scorpion ready to strike and scoffed, "I wanna know what you're doin' here. What are you in here for?"

Something in me snapped. "I was raped," I said loudly in her surprised face. "That's right, raped." I jumped out of my seat, feeling suddenly empowered by my own boldness. "You tried to take your life. I fought for mine. I looked death in the face, and I survived. And I'm going to make it. Because I'm not blaming society for what happened to me. I'm just looking to God and trying to go on with my life. And if you're smart, you will, too."

I sat down, shaking, shadowing my eyes with my hands, head bowed. I hadn't planned to jump up and counter her with my story. It was as if a force had come over me—a strength that I hadn't felt for months.

And then a strange thing happened. I looked up, and in front of me was a big, awkward but outstretched hand. I looked into her face, which had softened, and I saw that her eyes were filled with tears. "I had no idea," she said.

I smiled slightly and tentatively took her hand. "Forgiven and forgotten," I offered.

I had taken another step toward recovery. When I left that room, my terror subsided. The tremor in my right hand lessened, and for the first time in months, I was hungry. I got bolder, feistier, and a little more outspoken.

With this newfound respect from my therapy group, I was looked to as a leader—someone with guts, a role I recognized from my recent past. I noticed that everyone sat around and watched television all day. No one exercised or even walked much. Then they would complain that they were getting fatter, which would make them more depressed. There was one large sitting room where we would all assemble. As usual, the TV was blaring, and everyone was staring like zombies at the screen.

"You people have to get moving," I said. I jumped up and turned off the TV and flipped on the radio. Before they could object, I started dancing in the middle of the room. The song was "Maniac" from the movie *Flashdance*, ironic considering our place of containment. The words blasted, "She's a maniac, maniac on the floor. And she's dancing like she's never danced before."[1]

They formed a circle around me and started clapping and urging me to keep it up. The performer in me had returned. As I looked around at the faces, the words to the song seemed to fit all of us: "On the ice-blue eye of sanity, it's a place most never see."

I had lived in that place for a week now with these people. We shared a special bond, a bond that united victims and fellow sufferers—a bond of collective terror, collective anxiety, and collective anguish. The song continued, "Never stopping with her head against the wind. She's a maniac on the floor. And she's dancing like she's never danced before."[2]

"Let's see you do thirty more jumping jacks," someone called to me. "Look, she's doing it. Way to go!"

"Join in," I challenged. To my surprise, several did. Clapping, singing, and laughing surrounded us.

Suddenly, I heard from my roommate, "Susan, your doctor wants to speak with you." I stopped abruptly and turned around. I saw my doctor, watching my whole dance routine in the hallway. I hurried toward him, not knowing what to expect.

"I don't need the roof to fall in on me," he said. "I know you are stronger and on your way to recovery. You can go home now."

Never was I so happy to obey a doctor's order. I made arrangements for my departure and packed quickly. I said good-bye to my fellow patients and told them to keep praying and keep dancing. I felt a strange sense of sadness and despair, not knowing if they would all make it.

It has been said that compassion is feeling your pain in my heart. I had developed compassion in that hospital. I walked out that door and never looked back. Behind me, I heard the doors lock, blocking out the bustling noise of hospital activity. I stepped out into the noonday sun and felt its penetrating rays on my pallid face. I was free.

My hands were steady. My walk was brisk. And I vowed I would never be a victim again.

5

The Dance of Anger

"Locking rhythms to the beat of her heart, changing woman into life. She has danced into the danger zone when a dancer becomes a dance."[1]

It was my fifth aerobic class that day, and I still felt tense, tight, and angry. I knew that the only way I could sleep that night was to take one more class. But my legs were aching, my back was sore, and my feet were ready to fall off. I was in that danger zone that the song predicted. But I kept going. *Just one more class.*

I watched as the tiny beads of sweat trickled down my face and grew to large drops, forming pools of wetness on the new aerobic floor. My eyes then focused on the all-too-telling mirror, revealing a pinched leotard and an exposed bra strap. What surprised me was my expression. The mirror reflected a tense face, rigid except for an occasional wince of pain and wisps of hair that escaped the taut headband.

I used to love to dance and sweat and do aerobics. But now, I looked so grim. I looked like I wanted to punch someone—like I wanted to fight. I was fighting. But who was I fighting? God? Myself? The rapist? The gossips? Victimization? An unfair world?

Again, I turned to my reflection in the mirror. I was toned to the bone, and my bones were palpable. Three rows back, I

37

could count my ribs. I was living back in Boston now, and my journey to Massachusetts and all that I had gone through had taken its toll.

Before I had left the West Coast, my detective had nabbed my assailants, who had been identified in a lineup by the other two women at the dance studio. I hadn't been absolutely convinced, a fact that had greatly concerned my detective. But, as ordered, I had kept my eyes closed during the rape and had only caught one glimpse of the assailants as they had burst through the door.

As it turned out, my two assailants were part of that gang of six that had burst into the home of the father and son watching *Monday Night Football*; the six had raped the man's wife and her two girlfriends. It was also rumored, though to my knowledge never confirmed, that the six rapists were members of the larger, notorious gang, Bloods, often paired with their arch rivals, the Crips. Whenever the press would write about their repugnant rivalry, retaliations, and initiation rites, the two would usually be paired together—the Crips and Bloods. A mere mention of their menacing movements and crime sprees would muster fear in the most macho man.

The wife and mother of the football pair was a beautiful, auburn-haired woman, who was fearless at the lineups. She walked right up on the stage where the alleged criminals stood behind glass and carefully studied each one. Her husband and son accompanied her to every lineup as did the husbands of the other two women. The three women would actually make jokes while I sat there, cowering in fear and totally mute.

I wondered if the support that they received from their families made their recovery easier. They seemed to bounce back quicker than I did as an out-of-state, single woman. I think that their resilience after such a humiliating experience was due, at least in part, to love and support.

I was in Boston when the trial took place. Because so many other victims came forward to identify these creeps, I was not forced to return to California for the trial. I wasn't there physically, but I wasn't forgotten. The assailants were sentenced to two two-hundred-year, back-to-back sentences with no parole. After the verdict, the auburn-haired beauty waited until they brought the ringleader with the piercing eyes around the corner. She kicked him twice, right where it hurts, and said, "The first one is from me, and the second one is from the little blond in Boston."

Before I left California, my detective urged me to stay to give the West Coast a second chance. He tried to tempt me by reading a New England weather report. It was May, and it was snowing in Boston.

"I'm a hearty New Englander, and I'm great at shoveling snow," I bragged. "I just can't handle looking into the barrel of a gun. What happened to me in California? Well, those kinds of things just don't happen in Massachusetts."

Those words would haunt me when I read the Boston papers. Though I felt safer in my hometown, I returned to sensational headlines: the Big Dan rape trial, involving a gang rape on a pool table, and the Holbrook Five trial of teenagers accused of raping a retarded girl. But I didn't respond to the terrifying tabloid headlines with fear. Instead, I was furious. Rage, burning rage, had replaced my terror as I read these stories.

And then there was the nurse, Debby Smith. Gruesome details of Debby's demise were revealed at the trial of her murderers and recounted in all the newspapers.

The evening shift at a local hospital proved to be Debby's last. Exhausted from her night's labor, Debby returned to her Commonwealth Avenue apartment in Boston to get a few hours of well-deserved sleep. It was one o'clock on a sunny afternoon. While Debby slumbered, two burglars entered her apartment. Startled by a strange noise, she awoke to a knife against her throat. Quickly, they blindfolded her and then proceeded to disrobe her. In the struggle, the blindfold slipped.

"Open your eyes, and you're dead," one of them growled.

In that split second of naked terror that only a crime victim can fathom, Debby blinked. And for probably the first time in his life, the robber kept his word and slashed her throat. There but for the blink of an eye ... I, too, had been given that order. But unlike Debby, I had kept my eyes shut.

Debby blinked. I hadn't. One small, involuntary, reflex action accomplished in a fraction of a second meant Debby's death. It had been my life preserver.

But staying alive meant that I not only had to suffer through all the painful stages of rape recovery but the spurious, prurient gossip that followed me when I transferred back East with the same company. I had arrived at my new office filled with hope and excitement. I had wanted to put the rape and its aftermath behind me and pretend that it had never happened. I needed to start fresh with a clean slate. But they wouldn't let me.

The executives all told their assistants, "There is a young woman coming here from the West Coast office who was brutally raped. Of course, I am telling you this confidentially."

Yeah, right. The word had spread like wildfire before I even walked through the door. Cruelty comes in many forms: the barrel of a gun and the burning tongues of bored, brainless, boorish beings. Like vultures on a feeding frenzy, they savored every verbal morsel.

It had reached an apex one day when we were all called into a meeting. A senior vice president addressed the group, saying, "There is a very serious matter that you all need to be aware of. A woman was raped last night on the bike trail in back of our building." All heads turned toward me, eyes penetrating like lasers, looking for a reaction, waiting for me to unravel. The senior vice president continued to say, "The good news is that though she was raped, she wasn't hurt."

My insides cringed. *You can't be raped without being hurt, you Philistine.* After work that day, I went to the gym and took three aerobic-dance classes. Still livid after the day's events, I hit the inside track, running six miles until I collapsed in tears.

No matter what goals I achieved or what I accomplished, I was branded as "the rape victim." I decided that I needed to search for another position in another company. I found one quickly.

On my last day, my assistant took me out for a drink and confirmed all my suspicions about the insidious gossip. "Every day in the lunchroom," she told me, "they would talk about the nightly television soap operas and then talk about you. And you were real. They would say things, such as, 'Didn't she look depressed today? Really, she can't be normal. You can't go through a thing like that and be normal.'" Though my career suffered when I left this blue-chip company, cruel and ceaseless gossip made it impossible to stay.

No wonder that anger was, for me, the most prolonged stage of my recovery. My psychiatrist said that I had already suffered through the first stages of shock, denial, and fear. Without realizing it, I was following each stage sequentially, which most rape victims did, he said. I learned that this was healthy; what was unhealthy, my psychiatrist said, was lingering over a stage or never completing it, never moving on. He said that people varied widely in the ways they navigated the stages of recovery. Sadly, some turned to alcohol or drugs to get rid of the fear and anger. Others alienated family and friends. Still others, like me, got compulsive.

Even before the rape, a bad day at work never drove me to the bars to drink away my stress. Instead, I always exercised. So I wasn't surprised that I turned to aerobics and dance to get rid of the incredible anger that I felt. I took five or six classes a day. One time, I figured that I had done a thousand jumping jacks in the course of a night.

Anger propelled me. It drove me to my home away from home—to the ubiquitous spot that supplanted bars, singles' dances, gourmet clubs, and progressive dinners as "the place to be"—the health club.

In the beginning, health clubs were called gyms, and gyms were dark, dingy places where men in ratty sneakers played basketball, punched each other playfully, and told off-color jokes. Few women were seen in these places. Health clubs, on the other hand, featured carpeted spas, high-tech equipment, colorful decor, and juice bars. Men and women looked good as they worked out in two-hundred-dollar warm-up suits, spandex tights, shorts, and matching accessories.

It was the fad that gripped the times and still continues—the fitness craze. But it became more than a fad; it became part of the culture. The American dream of shaping our own destiny extended to our own bodies. Spawned by the "me" generation in their relentless pursuit of perfection, fitness became the new crusade, and it produced aerobic types determined to be perfect and devoted to the gospel of youth, beauty, and thinness. *Perfect.* There was even a movie with this title as Hollywood and Madison Avenue joined hands to promote the faces and bodies that they wanted us to possess. The pursuit of perfection swelled the coffers of the fitness clubs and created new fanatics and new victims. Each had a story.

There was Sally. Tall, slender, Nordic-looking, and always smiling, she was everyone's favorite aerobics instructor. She really seemed to care about her students, and they idolized her. But Sally had her secret. "Two years ago, I weighed two hundred pounds. I live in constant fear that I will lose control and get my old body back. You see, if I eat one cookie, I usually finish the whole box. So I keep an old picture of myself inside my tape case. I look at it often. It makes me exercise harder and longer."

And then there was Jeanie. Quietly, almost furtively, she entered the locker room. Her appearance was nondescript except for her emaciated frame. She spoke to no one, and no one noticed her. She changed quickly and then slipped into the bathroom. Alone in the stall, she stuck her finger down her throat and made herself vomit. She emerged with her head down and sullenly headed for class.

Kathy cloistered herself in the far corner of the aerobics room. Ten to fifteen years older than the other class members, she tried to keep up with the young dancers, who effortlessly lifted their limbs overhead. They were trying to avoid the beginnings of cellulite; Kathy was contemplating a "tummy tuck."

"Control it." "Tough it out." "Let it burn." These were some of the colloquial expressions that summed up a culture. Too often, sadly, that culture ended up twisting the real virtues of athletic endeavor—discipline, health, emotional release—into a narcissistic drive for human perfection.

I, too, was part of this culture. But after the rape, my priorities changed. Once driven to the pursuit of perfection, I was now using my physical workouts to maintain my sanity. My striving now became a will to live—a frantic quest to transcend the pain. The obsessive fervor, the addiction, the competitive streak, an athletic test of mind and body now became a Herculean effort to release my anger, cope with life's unfair blows, accept my fate, pick up the pieces, and go on living. I was, literally, dancing for my life!

Primed with an arsenal of angry thoughts, I felt like an alien in my daily aerobic classes with my fellow dancers. Shackled by relentless memories and unrestrained rage, my dance was a mélange of motion. Throbbing deep behind my intense, haunted eyes lurked the nightmare always at the marrow of my fury.

I couldn't stop working out until I was soaking wet. Then, after about five hours, I limped to the locker room, stumbled into the shower, and, still clammy in new sweats, trudged home—a somber silhouette against the flashy backdrop of the health club's neon sign.

I knew it was wrong. I knew it was excessive. If gluttony was a sin, then five or six hours of aerobics had to be frowned upon by the Almighty. I put my workouts before everything and everyone. It was the only thing that seemed to quell my rage.

This expression of physical anger was a catharsis, ridding me of my emotional pain and misery—a critical instrument in my healing. Counseling advocated that the healthiest response to adversity was to let it out: all the pain, the anger, the stress. That way, it wouldn't come back to plague you years later.

I did my battle with my demons on the dance floor. My diatribe was done in rhythm, and my questions, accusations, and tirades were all done to the beat. It would always happen in the middle of class when my body was in sync with the choreographed routine. My mind would turn to my predicament, and I would question God.

Why did this happen to me? What did I ever do to deserve such a fate? And God, where were you that night when I was being degraded? If you're a loving God, how could you look on while I was tortured? I need to know.

Very often, amid high-impact kicks, jumping jacks, and triple turns, I would start to feel in control. The more vulnerable I felt physically, the calmer I became mentally. It went something like this:

"Do fifty jacks. Count out loud; now, counting down. Forty-nine, forty-eight—"

God, you could have prevented the rape.

"Forty, thirty-nine, thirty-eight—"

Susan, don't confuse God with the evil actions of individuals. Bad things happen to innocent people. Go on with your life. Go forward.

"Thirty, twenty-nine, twenty-eight—"

But I'm so mad. I'm so angry. I can't forget. How can I go on?

"Twenty, nineteen—"

Persevere. Like an athlete in training, now, you feel the pain, the rigor, the hardship. But see the goal in sight—the goal attained.

One time during these exchanges, my shoe lacing became untied. It was just after a particularly stinging outburst when I screamed to myself, *God, you're so unfair. Why did you pick me to be raped? And if it had to happen, why didn't you just let me die?*

As I knelt down and crouched over the pesky lace, it came to me. I survived for a reason not yet known to me. I was spared, and it wasn't a mistake. At that moment, I was convicted. Bitter tears stung my face and wet my shoes as I remained kneeling while the dance class whirled around me.

This unorthodox form of venting, which paired the physical and the spiritual, might, on the surface, have appeared irreverent. But on my knees, I was too fearful to challenge God. On the dance floor, we wrestled, and I vacillated between anger and acceptance.

I had been told that people who suffered often swung back and forth with their emotions. I was no different in this regard. I alternately praised God for my survival but then blamed him for the painful memories that wouldn't subside. The question of how to be a decent person and live a good life in the aftermath of rape was a challenge.

The struggle of living a good life is often paralleled with the life of an athlete. Countless books and movies compare and contrast athletic endeavors with life's strivings. One of the most moving of these films, *Chariots of Fire*, is a feature film about Eric Liddell, the "Flying Scotsman," who set a world record and won a gold medal in the 1924 Paris Olympics. Later, he became a missionary in China. Revered worldwide, Eric often compared running a race to living one's life. Though only one person received first prize, he related, everyone ran to win. To win, you had to deny yourself many things that would prevent you from doing your best. Forgetting the past, you had to run straight to the goal with purpose in every step and strain to reach the end of the race.

In retrospect, perhaps my method of overcoming adversity wasn't so avant-garde after all. Though I questioned God, yelled at him, and challenged him, never once did I turn my back on him. God continued to be present in my healing process, even on the dance floor.

I continued with my excessive aerobics for several months. Then, one day, it happened—the nightmare of every dancer and athlete. Running for a bus, I tripped over a curb and fell. Excruciating pain shot through my ankle. I had wrenched my foot in three places—the ankle bone, the instep, and the heel. The doctor told me that I had to stay off it completely for at least three weeks. Hopefully, I had just sprained it.

I thought that I would go insane. I was used to doing thirty-five hours of aerobics a week, and now, nothing. My stress increased noticeably. My insomnia returned. My temper often flared. I felt like a caged animal.

I thought my foot was better after two weeks, so I decided to return to class. I only intended to take one class my first day back. But the music was intoxicating, so I decided to go on to the second and then to the third.

That night when I got home, I noticed a golf-ball-sized pocket of swelling on my left ankle. I iced it and then went to bed feeling apprehensive.

I was to leave the next day on a grueling ten-day business trip. There would be no time for exercising. I cheered up, thinking that when I returned, my ankle would be normal. But the swelling never healed, even when I stopped dancing. And the pain was increasing.

I saw another doctor, who told me, "You probably have torn all the ligaments in your ankle. We can't tell with X-rays. We will have to operate. Your dancing days are over, that's for sure."

I was stunned. I sought another opinion. "It looks like your ligaments are torn. We will have to do arthroscopic surgery and survey the damage. You'll have to find a more sedentary hobby. Consider sewing."

This can't be. God, you can't take away my dance. What will I do? I need it.

I went to eight doctors. Though their methods of operating varied, the prognosis was the same: "You will never dance again."

6

Forgiveness: The Signature Piece

The emblem of an era is its signature dance. Every decade ushers in a new dance genre—a signature piece that defines the times. The twenties, for example, had the Charleston, the thirties, the fox-trot, the forties, the swing, and the fifties, the jitterbug. We reminisce about these eras through the music and the dance that seemed to shape their spirit. These art forms serve as historical cornerstones to jog our memories and dust off the cobwebs of the years gone by.

Forgiveness is the cornerstone of recovery—the signature piece of a healed human being. The miraculous power of forgiveness restores life to the damaged person, once a sorrowful emblem of suffering. Forgiveness is not a human act; it is a superhuman act. Allowing unforgiveness to fester prevents a victim from moving forward. Charles Swindoll, in his book *Improving Your Serve*,[1] offers an amazing example of forgiveness when he relates a story about a young man he calls Aaron.

In the story, Aaron prayed that God would give him an important position helping others. But as time passed, Aaron realized that he would have to take any job he could find to replenish his finances. The only position available was as a bus driver on the South Side of Chicago. Aaron would be a rookie in a dangerous section of the city.

A gang of hoodlums discovered the new driver and tried to intimidate him. Four days in a row, they got on and walked right past him without paying, despite his warnings.

The next day, the gang got on as usual. But Aaron saw a policeman on the corner, pulled over, and reported the incident. The officer boarded the bus and told the boys to pay or get off. They paid, but unfortunately, the officer then disembarked. When the bus turned the corner, the gang attacked Aaron.

When Aaron came to, he was on the floor of the bus, bleeding profusely. Two teeth were missing, both eyes were swollen, and his money was gone. Anger, disillusionment, hurt, and resentment—all added fuel to the fire of his intense physical suffering.

Aaron decided to press charges. With the aid of the officer who had encountered the ruffians, most were rounded up and taken to the county jail. A hearing was scheduled.

When Aaron walked into the courtroom on the day of the hearing, the thugs glared at him, seething with anger. But as he looked at them, something strange happened. Suddenly, he was seized with new thoughts and compassionate feelings. His heart went out to the boys who had abused him. Instead of hating them, he pitied them. They needed help, not more hate.

When a verdict of guilty was pronounced, Aaron surprised the courtroom by requesting permission to speak. "Your Honor, I would like you to total up all the days of punishment for these men—all the time sentenced—and I request that you allow me to go to jail in their place." The courtroom was stunned. Aaron turned and looked at the gang members and said, "It is because I forgive you."

The judge finally spoke, "Young man, you're out of order. This sort of thing has never been done before!"

Aaron was not granted his request, but he did visit the gang members in prison. And he began working with other street kids in Chicago's South Side. The very thing he prayed for evolved from the pain of abuse and assault.

To forgive. It's such a small, concise, phrase—nine letters. It sounds so simple, but it is so difficult to do. For someone hurt badly, it seems impossible.

For me, forgiveness was the hardest requirement of recovery. Scarred and deeply wounded by all that had happened, I responded to my pain by escaping into excessive activity. I was left injured, still broken, and desperate—desperate for the peace and the serenity that eluded me.

Unforgiveness is frozen anger coiled in bitterness and resentment. It is as stifling as a muffled scream and a voiceless cry. It is an awesome feeling of helplessness and hurt, a trapped feeling worse than death itself. Encased in an ugly shell of unforgiveness, I was miserable. The aftermath of rape had left schisms in my relationships. I was still livid with the rapist and filled with debilitating hate for all criminals. And deep within—submerged in guilt—I still felt anger toward God.

I was now at an impasse. I was choreographed into a corner, and to move upstage, I had to choose a direction. I could be angry and follow a stormy path, or I could forgive. I was ready to move upstage. I chose forgiveness.

Forgiveness is one of those rare instances in life when the divine meets frail humanity and the two interlock. Forgiveness is the power to reject bitterness and revenge in exchange for peace and serenity.

But some, like me, need to hit bottom before they will forgive. I got to the point where it was either the peace of forgiveness or the relentless disharmony of an unforgiving spirit.

I had to forgive the rapist. I knew that he was locked up three thousand miles away. I knew he was receiving earthly punishment. That was enough. My thoughts of revenge only harmed me. Again, I had to let go. I made an intellectual decision to forgive even if my emotions still pointed in the other direction. I frankly admit that this didn't happen overnight. It was a process aided by certain people who came into my life and through the stories they told.

One story was about solitary confinement—the "black hole." Intent on restraining and, at times, even breaking a person, solitary confinement is the most dreaded form of prison punishment. In total isolation, some die. Many go mad.

Concerned about such inhumane treatment, a friend of mine from my church wanted to visit a man locked in solitary confinement and reach out to him. With permission from the prison chaplain, my friend entered the black hole. He described the scene to me: "The stench just about knocked me out; it was a putrid combination of sweat, urine, and mildew. On the grimy, gray walls were blotches of peeling paint; a filthy, roach-infested floor served as a resting area for the meek-looking, bespectacled man before me. He seemed so harmless; it was difficult to understand that he had been placed here for causing trouble among other inmates. I had planned to discuss forgiveness with this gentle man, but he preempted our conversation by telling me that he wanted to explain why he was in prison."

"You see," the prisoner explained, "I molested my thirteen-year-old stepdaughter. But I know in my heart that God has forgiven me."

"I was sickened," my friend continued. "I also no longer wanted to help this man. Feeling guilty, I approached the prison chaplain and related the afternoon's events."

"I can understand how you feel," the chaplain said. "But try giving it one more chance. After all, if you didn't believe that an individual can be reformed, you wouldn't be here. If God can forgive him, can't you?" Next day, my friend returned to the black hole. And he returned days and weeks after that.

More help for my unforgiveness came from a testimony I heard one night at church from a former prisoner. This man had been sent to jail for a year on trumped-up charges. He questioned his circumstances but came to the conclusion that there had to be a master plan. After entering the penitentiary, he worked with the chaplain, sharing his vision of forgiveness with the other felons. The chaplain and this inmate were amazingly successful at counseling and guiding the other prisoners. After spending a year of his life incarcerated, the charges were dropped. This man had been falsely accused of rape.

His vision of forgiveness resonated with me. He said, "The final stage of forgiveness is to give away a part of yourself—to reach out to others with love and acceptance. What one person does for another is what's going to ignite and impact a whole lot of people. So get outside yourself. And forgive."

Something else about this man's story also helped me move toward forgiveness. He was black. The man who raped me was black, too. And though I had solid relationships with black friends from church and work, seeing young blacks in garb similar to what my assailants wore that night brought out a fear I couldn't control.

But my fear was dissipated in a truly miraculous way.

Crippled by my ankle injury and distraught over the doctors' prognoses of never dancing again, I gave up any hope of recovery until a friend recommended a surgeon who was a basketball player and a skier—a consummate athlete. He had studied in Switzerland and had operated on injured members of the ski team.

I figured one more medical visit couldn't hurt. After all, this would up the tally to nine doctor bills. This doctor was different, however. Instantly, we had the mutual respect and rapport of fellow athletes. He understood how important dance and aerobics were to me.

"Doctor, if I have to give up dancing forever, my life won't be the same," I tried to explain. "Dancing gives me such joy, and it relieves stress."

"I know, I know," he said. "You don't need to recite the benefits. I recite them daily to my more sedentary patients. There is a surgery that I've performed that may work for you. But it has some risks and drawbacks."

"What are they?" I asked.

"The operation is very painful," the doctor said. "I drill a hole through your ankle bone and pull the ligaments through. When the sedation wears off, the pain is excruciating. You will need a morphine drip to get through it. Also, the repair may only last for five years. The ligaments may loosen and stretch, and we may need to operate again. Also, the recovery time is long and includes three to four months in a cast and after that, a cane and months of physical therapy. But if it works, there is a good chance that you will dance again."

I felt totally safe in this doctor's hands. I was sure that he was sent from above. He was gentle, soft-spoken, compassionate, brilliant ... and black. If I had been brutalized and raped by black felons, God, in his wisdom and providential care, saw to it that a talented, black doctor would put me back together again. My torn ligaments would be fused by the hand of man but healed by the touch of God.

The date for the operation was set. The doctor gave me a brace to wear. It held what was left of my foot in place. The day before the operation, he checked me over one more time and said, "Don't eat or drink anything, even water, after midnight. And you should be at the hospital by ten in the morning."

I had a sudden thought. "Doctor," I asked him, "if I ran—or even danced—while wearing this brace, could I further damage this foot?"

"No, all the ligaments are torn already," he answered. "You couldn't damage it any further. Why do you ask?"

"Oh, no reason."

The night before the operation, I prepared myself by pretending that I was going on a trip. I packed and primped by painting my toenails, having a bubble bath, and catering to myself to avoid reality. But I awoke early the next morning with a sense of dread. *What if the operation doesn't work? What if my ankle gets worse? What if ...*

I took the brace from the nightstand and buckled its awkward straps to my reddening calf, tightly securing my ankle region. I limped to the other room, searching frantically for the blue and white monstrosity that contained a huge part of my life—my workout bag. Rifling through its contents like a woman possessed, I gave no thought to style or color or matching socks. Somehow, I got dressed and then ventured out into the cold November morning, pulling my parka over my skimpy attire.

My car stalled incessantly. But still, I wouldn't give up. With breakneck speed, I pulled into the parking lot of the health club. I waved the customary card in front of the receptionist.

Clumsily stripping off my bulky winter coat, I stopped abruptly, almost crashing into one of my regular classmates as she headed toward me. "Hi, Susan, what's your hurry? Want a sip of water?" She handed me her water bottle.

"No, thanks," I responded, "I'm fasting."

I decided to take an early morning aerobic-dance class before the operation. Yes, it was crazy. But my doctor had said that I couldn't do any more harm. And I had resigned myself to a long recovery and the possibility that this might be my last dance.

Ten minutes before the end of class, I grabbed my workout bag and hurried home. A quick shower, and then my girlfriend arrived to take me to the hospital. There was no time for nerves.

Admission was accomplished in record time, and before I knew it, I was donning a green, loose-fitting garment, worn by many surgical patients. They even gave me matching green, paper slippers for my wheelchair ride down to the operating room. In pre-op, they moved me to a gurney, and a nurse monitored my vital signs. A few minutes after that, they wheeled me into the operating room. My doctor and several other medical personnel, also attired in this hospital green, swarmed around me, each performing his or her particular task on various parts of my anatomy.

"We're going to give you a shot to make you sleepy before we finally put you out with anesthetic," said my doctor.

I felt the prick, and then I started feeling very drowsy and mellow. All that green was becoming blurry. But I could still hear their pre-op chatter. "Oh no!" someone in green exclaimed. "We're in trouble. She has toenail polish on all ten toes." So much for my primping the night before. I didn't realize that scrubbing for an operation included the removal of nail polish.

I finally felt myself going under. But before I did, I found my doctor's hand and grabbed it. I raised my heavy eyelids, and the last words that my parched mouth uttered were, "Sorry, I was just trying to be well-groomed."

7

New Steps for a New Life

I t starts in the womb. Just ask their moms. Their kicks have
extra oomph! As infants, they crawl rhythmically. Their first
step is a two-step. Before they walk too far, they try to twirl.
They are part human, part artist, part ham. They are dancers.

I was one of those twirling toddlers. In old home movies, I'm
dancing my way into the hearts of anyone who applauded. My
younger brother stared in drooling wonder at such boldness.

One day, at the tender age of six, I was flipping the television
dial and suddenly saw them. In an ornate ballroom, dominated
by a crystal globe that refracted the light and scattered it across
the stage, danced two glamorous creatures. Elegantly, they glided
into my living room, changing my life forever.

Fred and Ginger.

The mere mention of this dazzling duo conjured up images
of class, style, finesse, and chic. The perfect blending of the
music and their movement was like champagne—sparkling to
the surface for a few golden moments.

Whirling through a celluloid eternity of magic, Astaire and
Rogers piqued the imagination of a star-struck child. With rapt
attention, I studied their long-limbed command of rhythm and

space and their use of eloquent gestures to render so vividly the splendor of romantic love.

It was an excursion into enchantment.

And I was easily enchanted! I secretly spent hours in front of the mirror, mimicking the moves of the masters and dreaming of the day when I would dance with distinction.

Eagerly, I read books on dance from its genesis to modern-day genres. I learned that dance has existed since the beginning of time as ritual, as recreation, as spectacle, as custom, and even as worship. Many choreographers have commented on the spiritual side of dance. Twyla Tharp once said, "Dance represents the God in me." "Only God can create. Man can only assemble what is out there," claimed ballet choreographer George Balanchine. "Dance is worship," said Agnes de Mille. "Dance is the hidden language of the soul," said Martha Graham.[1]

Simply put, dance is a very high art. Dancers wordlessly demonstrate every facet of human emotion. Dance inspires and transforms the commonplace. It can transport both dancer and audience into another world—a world of transcendent wonder and beauty.

But dance is also tremendously physical—an athletic endeavor. To dance well requires that mind, spirit, and body work in concert. That total involvement was what I loved most about dance. It is art performed by an athlete.

And it was that athletic angle that occupied my attention one long afternoon. Sprawled in my chair with my foot in its heavy cast propped up in front of me, I watched the afternoon movie *Singin' in the Rain*, starring one of my favorite dancers, Gene Kelly.

If Fred Astaire was the sine qua non of suave in the 1930s, then Gene Kelly electrified the 1940s with a daring, athletic dance style that became his hallmark. Muscular and casual in a striped T-shirt, a sailor suit, or even a raincoat, Kelly managed to imbue every number with powerful grace. And with his crooked grin and Midwestern accent, he showed that dance was for everybody, not just artistic types.

Kelly's dance style was rooted in his lifelong belief that dancing and athletics were inextricably linked. In 1956, in a televised special titled *Dancing: A Man's Game*, he set out to illustrate that conviction. Assembling a few of the world's greatest sportsmen, Kelly showed that most dance movements had their athletic equivalent on the gym floor or playing field. And he maintained that the only difference between sport and dancing was that one was competitive and the other creative.

Gene Kelly foreshadowed the future when a new blend of dance steps and cardiovascular training became the rage. Dancers were the first to recognize that their art fit the requirements of aerobic conditioning and that adding music and choreography made exercise more enjoyable. People flocked to the new classes. I eagerly joined.

For me, aerobic dance combined the best of both worlds—my love of dance and my competitive athletic streak. The dance, with its choreographed steps, satisfied my yen for variety, while the aerobics gave me a natural athletic high, which made me smile during class. This caught the eye of many teachers. They didn't always know my name, but they knew me as "the one who smiles" in a class where everyone else was grimacing. Dance and movement always gave me such joy.

"I'm singin' and dancin' in the rain," crooned Gene Kelly from my TV. He swung around a lamppost with such infectious joie de vivre that I longed to get up and join him. But my eyes wandered from the screen to the cast, a grim reminder of reality.

I was home from the hospital and recuperating for two months. I spent my time watching old Hollywood musicals and wondering if I would ever dance again. The movie ended; I clicked it off. I shifted uncomfortably—what next?

Listlessly, I picked up a case of cassette tapes from the table next to me, a gift from a visiting colleague who thought it would inspire me. I selected a tape at random, dropped it in the player, pushed the Start button, and experienced the first in a cascade of surprises.

I knew that voice—from long ago! Time, which often dulls the luster of memories, graciously took a holiday as I sat there listening, and my mind turned back the clock.

When I was an energetic, exuberant child, I never expected to be singled out for any particularly dramatic experience. I do remember, though, that I yearned for an exciting future. Sometimes at night, gazing at the stars, I felt certain that something extraordinary was going to happen to me. I had one surpassing goal: I did not want to be ordinary.

I attended a parochial primary school with three of my cousins: Linda, my age, and our older cousins, Mike and Billy. The boys called Linda and me little brats and vacillated between protecting us and playing practical jokes.

Just before Christmas, Mike and Billy and their friend Tom took me aside and said, "Sister Mary Geraldine will ask if you know any Christmas carols, and we are going to teach you one so that you will be Sister's favorite."

I eagerly listened and memorized the words.

Next day in class, Sister asked us, "Children, does anyone know the words to any Christmas carol?" I was the only one to raise my hand. "Susan, which carol do you know?"

"'The First Noel,' Sister."

"Well, why don't you sing it for the class?"

Concentrating on the words I had been taught, I belted out, "Noel, Noel, Noel, Noel. We ain't got no water 'cause we ain't got no well."

I was kept after school till Easter.

The boys thought it was hysterical, especially Tom. This was one of their worst practical jokes. But I would get them. I vowed revenge.

I got my chance the next day. We were all playing a game of hide-and-seek. Linda and I had to choose whether we wanted to be on Mike's or Billy's team. Fickle and finicky, we both said that we wanted Billy. Tom turned to me and said, "If you choose Mike, you'll be my best friend."

"Who cares," I snapped triumphantly.

My mother, it seemed, came out of nowhere and smacked me. "Couldn't you be nice to that boy and do what he asked?"

Tom corrected her, "Don't punish her. She treats me like Mike and Billy. I like that."

What has happened to Tom since we were young? He is a film and television actor; an athlete, who holds two national-championship records in wrestling; a musician; and an author. He earned a degree from Harvard in clinical psychology. He runs six miles a day. He skydives (with thirty-seven jumps on his record). He swims. And he's blind.

Though blind since childhood, Tom refused to be a victim. He participated in normal childhood games, including playing hide-and-seek with fresh little girls.

When I was in college, I went with a group of friends to a club to hear a new musician. Appearing for the first time was Tom. During intermission, I went up and reintroduced myself. To my chagrin, he blurted out, "Oh yeah, the little brat."

Trying desperately to cover my embarrassment, I asked, "Tom, how far do you plan to go with your music and writing?" "Right to the top!" was his instant reply.

The tape I was now listening to was that of Tom. He was addressing a Million Dollar Roundtable of five thousand insurance executives from around the world. The title of his speech: "Turning Your Disadvantage into an Advantage." Here are a few highlights:

"You've got a disadvantage? Take advantage of it. People don't buy similarity; they buy differences." Tom's voice on the tape advised. "That disadvantage is what makes you different—unique. Have you ever considered the impact your disadvantage would have on the world if you got out of your self-pity, took life by the throat, and became a message? What is your story?" asked Tom. "Everybody has a story. And most likely, there is some injustice in it. You think that's the thing that has caused you to become a failure. But I'm here to tell you it could very possibly be your message for life."[2]

I sat mesmerized. Despite Tom's remarkable talents, he probably wouldn't have an audience were he not blind. This struck a responsive chord with me. I believed that I, too, had a message. My life had changed radically in the three years since the rape. But I was still existing in a survival mode: surviving the rape, surviving a breakdown, surviving in my career, and now, trying to survive this operation and regain my dancing feet.

In my cherished book of quotes, I read that Henry Wadsworth Longfellow believed that nothing that happens with

God is accidental. I, too, held these beliefs. I survived for a reason. Perhaps the underside of the tapestry of my life was being created, weaving the many dark threads to distinguish the future brilliant hues on top. I wanted to believe that my day and my message would come and that I would make a difference to others who were hurting. I longed to believe that the brilliant hues would someday appear.

With my foot in its plaster cast plopped unceremoniously on the coffee table, I put aside my audio and video pursuits to catch up on my reading. I chose *The Hiding Place* by Corrie ten Boom. Though I knew the story of the Dutch woman's rescue of thousands of Jews and her subsequent internment in a concentration camp, I had never read her book. I was enthralled with the courage of Corrie and her family in the face of impending doom. One particular story vivified me.

Caught harboring Jews in their home, the Ten Boom family were taken to Gestapo headquarters. Alone with one Gestapo official, Corrie offered him her story. He ridiculed her and sent her away. But the next day, he sent for her. He said that he had been up all night, thinking about what she had said. He wanted to know more. Next, Betsie, Corrie's sister, entered for her inquisition. With great joy, she testified to her faith, and then she asked if she could pray with the Nazi. He agreed.[3]

And I thought, There they were—the prisoner with her judge—the victim with her victimizer. As I read those words, something stirred inside me. I felt a sudden rush, a kaleidoscope of thoughts, feelings, and fragmentary phrases from what I had read and heard. *Victim and victimizer ... prisoner and prison ... testimony ... message ... prayer ... changed lives ... disadvantage ... make a difference.* A muse of many voices resounded in my head.

Then it came to me. *Prison.* I could go into prison, like that man in my church, and work with criminals—not only to be sure that I had forgiven, but to tell them my story. To bring them the message that people can change. And I am living proof.

But doubt dampened my rising excitement. Why would they listen to me? From their point of view, I was still well off, successful, from another world. What would we really have in common? Discouraged, I picked up the book again. But snippets from Tom's tape kept swirling around in my head: *your disadvantage ... use it ... it makes you unique ... it is your message.*

Tom's disadvantage was his blindness. Mine was the rape and my subsequent struggle with fear and anger. But what was my unique message? Then it came to me—another epiphany. I remembered the promise I had made to God that I would try to do some good in this world, reach out to those less fortunate. Now, I knew how!

I could teach aerobic dance in a women's prison. Dance, exercise, and aerobics could be common denominators, shared interests. I could make exercise fun, using popular tunes with the newest dances. In doing so, I would help foster good relationships and show prisoners the benefits of a healthy lifestyle.

My exuberance was suddenly tempered once again, this time by the throbbing of my foot in its plaster prison, bringing me back to the real world of the moment. After a short period at home, I returned to work on crutches. Then came a brace and finally, a cane. My co-workers described me as the one who limped. I went to physical therapy three times a week for longer than I care to remember. But ever so slowly, the pain subsided, and my limp lessened, and I graduated from orthopedic shoes to respectable flats.

One day, I walked into my doctor's office for my usual visit. He proceeded with his usual manipulations of my foot while I mentally calculated my afternoon appointments. "You're ready."

"Ready for what?" I inquired.

"To go back."

"Back where?" I was puzzled.

My usually shy, reserved doctor took me by the shoulders, looked me in the eyes, and said, "Dance, girl. That's why we operated."

I couldn't believe it! Of course, I wouldn't know what my limitations would be until I tried. Maybe I would never get my full range of motion back. Maybe I would have too much pain. But I was determined to get back on the dance floor. I made immediate plans to join my favorite dance troupe at the next available class.

The day came. I was psyched. I walked into the studio, and there it was—the sweet smell of sweat. That night, I wouldn't have traded it for Parisian perfume. I strutted to the center of the locker room and announced at the top of my lungs, "I'm back!"

Shrieks. Giggles. Hugs. Dancing friends swarmed around me with various renditions of "Welcome back!"

"We've missed you." said one of my friends.

"Wait till you see our new numbers!" exclaimed another.

"Was it very painful?" another girl asked anxiously.

"Laid up all that time, and you didn't gain any weight!" remarked another.

"You look rested, peaceful," assured another. "Are you ready to really workout?"

I didn't know the answer to that one, yet. But I was about to find out. I slipped the athletic brace under my foot, wincing slightly. Quickly, I tied my shoes as I heard the music starting.

"I've been saving your spot," smiled my good friend Lori. We always stood beside each other.

I took my place beside her and then said to the teacher, "Let's dance to some of the old tunes. I want to see if I've still got it," I joked.

She accommodated. And I was in a state of euphoria. Although my foot felt strained, I felt no real pain. I thanked God profusely. I went home and iced it and rested. But I made plans to get together with the women from my church who were interested in my prison dance outreach.

My friend Polly, also a dancer, let us use her dream dance studio with an all-telling wall of mirrors. The mirrors helped us perfect our form, and since only one other instructor had dance experience, it helped me perfect the steps of the others.

After mastering all the dances, we quibbled about whether we would be able to teach the inmates choreography, such as, moving demi-plies, grapevines, quick spins across the floor, chassés, cold ducks, pelvic tilts, and hip sways, all encased in an aerobic framework. Should we teach them the vast vocabulary of the muscles they were using? Would they even want to know?

We decided that we would teach them clear structures and phrasing that would make them feel and look like dancers even if the steps weren't perfect. After all, we wanted them to have fun and get fit.

We met on the weekends. I choreographed most of our routines. We chose music that we thought the prisoners would enjoy. We also discussed the staging and the format of the class. We would start with aerobics set to popular tunes and then cool down with slower, calmer music. There would be time after class for chatting with the inmates, allowing them to share and voice any concerns. We decided that we would be ready to go into prison in one month. Since we were connected with the outreach ministries of our church, they prepared the inmates for our imminent arrival by word of mouth and with flyers that they put around the prison.

I was excited. Only one thing was troubling me. What would we call ourselves? What did I want to communicate to these very young, very troubled girls? What did I want to leave them with—what did I want to impart? Joy. I wanted to impart joy. Into the gruesome garrison that held these girls, I wanted to bring an hour of pure joy. We would call ourselves the Joy Dancers.

Since we had already decided to wear big T-shirts, we would have them inscribed "Joy Dancers" with two leaping women on the front. Name decided. Costumes ready. Everything in place. Curtain up!

◆   ◆   ◆

The slight, delicate-boned brunette called to her friend, "Come see the bulletin board outside the cafeteria, Sabrina."

Sabrina obliged. Hands on hips, eyes squinting, she read out loud, "Starting this Thursday night at seven o'clock, dance aerobics, taught by the Joy Dancers. The class is a series of choreographed numbers performed aerobically. Wear comfortable clothing. Great exercise! Great fun!"

"You should try it," the brunette said. "You love to dance."

"And I'm good," said Sabrina. "I bet I could show those Joy Dancers a thing or two."

"You need the exercise. You're starting to put it on!" said her friend.

"No way!" Sabrina playfully nudged her cell mate, and a giggling, girlish spat with pinches, slaps, and hair pulling ensued.

"Fight!" Two guards ran toward them, believing their playfulness to be a dangerous altercation. "Lockup for you two."

"But Sergeant," pleaded Sabrina, "we were just fooling around. We're best girlfriends."

"Then you won't mind being stuck with each other all night," said the guard. "Get moving."

8

Enter the Joy Dancers

B arbed wire: Razor-ribbon. Replica of restraint. Steely reminder of quarantine. Muted but malevolent mechanism of coiled confinement.

On this bitterly cold winter night, the barbed wire encircling the compound glistened as strands of icicles hung precipitously from its spirals. I shivered as I maneuvered my car up the long driveway. Police cars were lined up in columns, and guards walked briskly through the yard, tightly holding the reins of rather sinister-looking canines.

Why did I ever think this was going to work? What a lousy way to spend a Thursday night after a hard day of work. I must be crazy!

I turned off the ignition and tightened my jacket around my chest to hide the trembling. I noticed that my companions were wide-eyed and visibly shaken. "Group hug! This will work. We just need to get used to these surroundings."

We hugged each other, got out of the car, and walked past the police and the dogs. We entered a smoky, crowded waiting room, inhabited by scruffy-looking individuals there to visit female inmates.

All prison proceedings came to an abrupt halt and all eyes were on us—six pony-tailed women with pink headbands, matching leg warmers, aerobic shoes, and startling, colorful T-shirts adorned with black script.

"What do you call yourselves?" asked the short, beefy guard, face leathered from too much sun or too much stress.

"The Joy Dancers." I turned around to show him my T-shirt.

"That's different. We've never had anything like that in here," he said sarcastically.

"Bring in the aerobic people for pat down," bellowed the woman guard from the anteroom.

We entered a small enclosed area—the trap, they called it.

Two large, female guards faced us and ordered us up against the wall. The jowly guard focused on one of my instructors. "Do you have a weapon in your pocket? What is that sticking out?"

"It … it's my hip bone," she stuttered.

The guards looked at each other and burst out laughing. "We don't see many hip bones around here," she volunteered. Their faces seemed to soften, and the rest of the search went smoothly. The only caveat was that they could have correctly purchased bras for each of us.

"Extend your arms to the side," ordered the jowly guard. "Now, open your mouth. Lift up your right foot; now, your left. Do you plan to have a hole in your sock every week?"

I looked down, and peering through the pink terry cloth was my big toe. My face matched my socks.

We passed inspection, and as the guard turned the key, admitting us into the foyer of the jail, she said, "It will get easier each time. Trust me." She then pressed a buzzer and yelled, "Six for holding."

The holding area was the size of a roomy elevator with only one window peeking into the reception area. I paced nervously despite the limited space.

"Stand still. You're making us antsy," demanded one of my instructors.

"I can't help it," I said. "Plus, I need to use the bathroom."

"Well, you'd better tell the guard at the window," said my instructor, "because once inside, we're limited to the gym."

Reluctantly, I rapped on the window and told the guard my plight. Rolling his eyes in disgust, he came around and opened the holding door. I walked through a smoke-filled room where other visitors waited. Greasy, sleazy characters looked at me up and down in my conspicuous dance outfit. "Don't stare or say a word. She's from church," my guard accosted the curious onlookers, waving a jeweled hand with a gaudy ring on every finger. "And you, go to the bathroom before you leave home," he chastised me.

When I returned from the bathroom, he said to me, "Okay, back to pat down."

"But I've already been there," I protested.

"Sorry, you left holding. For all we know, you could have been hiding something in the restroom. It's the rule around here. No exceptions."

This night was getting very long, but I complied. Finally back in holding, we were let in. Clutching our aerobic tapes, pulling up our leg warmers, and fastening our headbands, we entered—prison.

Lock, double-lock, keys clanking all the way. We followed the guard down a long hall deep into the recesses of the institution. He turned left and opened the door to a large, musty gym where sixty women prisoners were waiting for us.

Walking to the front of the gym felt like running the gauntlet. Inmates in a defiant stance with arms folded and jaws set challenged our very existence. They looked us up and down, and we heard a host of taunts and jeers. "Look at them," one of the inmates said. "What do those shirts say?"

"Joy Dancers?" another jeered. "Get real."

"They're from church," said another inmate. "What can these church girls show us?"

I said to my instructors, "We're all cued up. Now, let's do it just as we rehearsed." Then I addressed the inmates. "Hi, ladies, we're the Joy Dancers. We've put together an aerobic-dance program that we hope is both fun and great exercise. Our songs are based on top-forty hits. Don't worry if you can't get all the steps tonight, because we'll be here every week. Is everybody ready?" Expectant hush. "Hit it. Walk front, touch left, and clap."

"Oh, I love this song. These church girls can really move," said one of the inmates.

After awhile, I said, "Now, we're going to learn a new dance. The first combination looks like this. Let's try it together slowly. Walk right for four and make that walk your own with hips, shoulders, shimmies, whatever you feel, and wherever the rhythm takes you. Now pivot right, then left. Now do it again on the left side. Can you pick up the tempo? I think you can. From the top, and give me some attitude—dance attitude, that is. Do you know what I mean, ladies?"

Chorus of: "Sure, Yeah, We get it."

Okay, let's try it. Great job, everybody!"

One of the guards came in. "Hey, what's going on in here?" he said.

"No problem, Sergeant," piped up one of the inmates. "We're just dancing."

They like it. They like the program. It's working.

"All right, time to cool down," I said. "Listen to the words and keep your movements slow and fluid." The girls mirrored my motions. After a few minutes, I said, "That's it, class. Thanks for coming. God bless you, and we'll see you next week. Practice our new routines."

Sixty women swarmed around us, praising all the instructors and hugging us like they didn't want us to leave. The guards gazed in wonder. This time, we didn't mind hearing their comments. "This is the best thing we've ever had here," said one of the inmates. "Are you really coming back next week?"

"I loved the dances," said another.

"Your shirts are cool," we heard from another inmate. "Are you going to get them for us? We want to be Joy Dancers."

Enjoying all the kudos, I barely noticed the three women who slowly stalked me and finally surrounded me. I found myself cut off from the rest of the class and the other instructors. *Oh God, I was warned about this. Please protect me.*

One woman, the ringleader, still perspiring heavily from class, moved nearer, eyeing me suspiciously. Her lips were pressed into thin lines of resistance. Her nostrils flared in breathy boldness. When she was so close that I could count the tiny beads of sweat on the grooves of her face, she halted, pointed a bony index finger at me, and said, "You know, you dance real good for a white girl!"

Relieved, I smiled broadly. "Thanks, that's one of the best compliments that I've ever received."

"Are you really coming back here next week?" the woman asked.

"I am."

"And the week after that?"

"Yes, and every week until summer starts," I assured her.

"Just like school—dance school."

"Hey, all you guys," she called. "Make way for the teach!"

I left there on cloud nine. But my jubilation was quickly quashed when a slimy male guard snarled, "Six pink shirts came in; make sure that only six leave."

"Yes, sir," said the female guard escorting us.

That was just the beginning. As the weeks wore on, we had similar experiences. Some of the guards appreciated volunteers and others wished all programs would be scratched. We also became more involved with the women as they confided in us. We did have our difficult times and difficult individuals. Some we won over, some we didn't. Most of the women were thrilled to have a dance class in prison.

The night of our second class, a burly woman with a shorn skull entered the gym. She scrutinized me with disgust and then voiced her opinion for everyone to hear. "This broad will never last in here. She looks like a wimp. Three, four weeks max she'll go crying back to the suburbs and figure she's done her one good deed in life."

With a sardonic smile, she folded her arms decisively and swaggered away. Months later, she approached me and said, "I've got to hand it to you; you're a lot tougher than you look. You really love doing this, and it shows. You look like a happy, excited little kid. And when we watch you and dance with you, we start feeling that way, too, even if it is just for an hour."

Another night, a rather rowdy group of women came in and took over. They wouldn't let us put the tapes in the recorder.

They were playing their own radio, singing, snapping their fingers, and sashaying around the gym like it was their turf.

"Let's get out of here," said one of my instructors. "They're looking for trouble."

One woman grabbed my tapes and then sat up on the table with the recorder, hugging it possessively. She leaned back slowly, her eyes narrowed, her lips drawn back sourly, exposing a glistening gold tooth. "Just what do you plan to do in here tonight?"

"Dance," I said. "We dance to choreographed routines."

"Is that church music?" she asked.

"No," I said, "you know the song that's playing on the radio right now that you seem to like so much? Well, that is on our class tape. And choreography is putting dance steps to a whole song, like you see on TV. Why don't you try it? You might like it. Would you mind putting my tape in the recorder?"

"Why not," she agreed. "I got nothing better to do."

"You can stand right in back of me, and then you can learn the steps to your favorite song," I suggested.

Extending a thin, flexed arm, she motioned for the rest of her gang to fall in line. They stayed for the whole class, but they never came back.

As the weeks wore on, I discovered that most of the inmates had been abusing their bodies with drugs and alcohol and had been mistreated by pimps and drug dealers. Some had been molested by family members, often since early childhood. No matter what the crime, they all had one thing in common—they were filled with self-hate. Their bodies were things to be used and abused.

I not only had to teach them to dance, I had to teach them to love themselves. A good place to start was with a healthy respect for the body—the temple of the soul.

Enter the Joy Dancers.

9

Tales of the Dance

M y purpose in starting the Joy Dancers was twofold. First, I wanted to provide an outlet for the prisoners' anger, stress, and violent propensities and, at the same time, help them form a better self-image. Second, I wanted to establish a common ground for communication—our love of dance.

Each week, as they got into better shape, I hoped that they would become more attuned with their own physicality and achieve a sense of accomplishment as they learned new dance routines. Through the aerobics program, their health would also benefit as their heart rates improved, their blood pressure and cholesterol levels normalized, and the pounds began to come off. A month after my first class, some of the inmates began doing aerobics on their own twice a week.

I quickly learned just how serious these women's physical needs really were. For women in their late teens and early twenties, most were in terrible shape. I saw the effects of drugs on both mind and body. They had trouble following a simple routine, and initially, they were not able to do a full twenty-minute aerobic segment. So much for the fancy footwork I had rehearsed with my instructors.

One night, as I was leading the second song, I happened to glance over my shoulder to see that most of the women were sitting in chairs around the gym, huffing and puffing. They were not able to get through two aerobic songs without stopping. I had to revamp our entire program, switching to easier movements and slower songs until they had built some endurance.

Excess weight was also a problem for many inmates. A combination of inactivity, greasy prison food, and an absence of unhealthy drugs had filled them out considerably. This contributed to their depression and poor body image.

But after a few weeks, we began to hear glowing reports about the weight they were losing, the dance steps they had perfected, and how they intended to continue with aerobics when they were freed.

Most were more than willing to work at the program for one reason—they loved to dance. We all shared a common love of music and movement. Dance brought us together—inmates and instructors—having fun, refining the craft, exercising, and building strength and endurance.

I also taught them a dancer's discipline—the discipline of a chorus line and a ballet barre. For most of the inmates, their dancing had consisted of a few rap steps with no particular sequence or choreography. An involved dance number or aerobic routine was out of their realm, but something they were very interested in learning. We taught them to memorize steps and routines and to move together in concert with others. These were disciplines that could be carried over to other areas of their lives.

As I had hoped, our classes provided an emotional outlet and a perfect antidote for "women in cages," as one inmate described their cells. Feeling confined, angry, and bitter, many inmates entered my class with skepticism, some with an attitude, and all with the scars from their past. I quickly came to recognize the many layers of pain behind their words and actions.

Anger. The acid of anger is perhaps the most powerful of all human emotions. It courses through a body, burning and destroying any positive emotion that tries to surface. Anger exists for a reason. It is a signal, a message that we are being hurt, our rights are being violated, our needs aren't being met, or our desires or ambitions are being thwarted.

The problem with anger is not its existence, but its expression. And that's where so many of the inmates got into trouble. They had no outlet for their inevitable anger—at their families, at the prison system, at society, at themselves. Most of them had no positive models for handling anger or ways of venting it.

I understood the power of anger all too well. There were times after the rape when I seethed with rage and almost lost control. But when I got angry, I always headed for the treadmill or the StairMaster to quell my fury. I hit the exercise machines or the dance floor. Many inmates hit someone else. The anger was the same; what differed was managing the anger—finding a nonviolent way to vent it.

My commitment was to teach the women to turn anger into a constructive force for reshaping their lives—to channel it into something that would benefit them instead of hurting them.

One inmate sat on the sidelines, nursing a broken leg. From a short distance, she looked like a man—tall and slim, wearing wrangler jeans and a baseball hat pulled down tightly over closely cropped hair. She watched the class every week with her arms folded. She had cold eyes and a sarcastic smirk. Something made me reach out to her. "Hi, I'm Susan." I stuck out my hand for her to shake.

"Why are you doing that?" she asked.

"Shaking hands is a way of getting acquainted. It is a sign of respect," I said.

She eyed me suspiciously. "I guess no one ever respected me before." She reluctantly offered a limp hand.

Sometimes, she would try to do some of the exercises from her seat. The other instructors were afraid of her. "Why do you talk to her?" one of them asked me. "I just wish she would go away; she's so mean-looking. We can't reach everyone, you know, and she looks like a troublemaker."

"You know, that's the truth," offered one of the inmates. "She's in here for life—murder. What a temper! She hit another woman over the head with a baseball bat."

But I knew I was no better than this inmate who had lost control and taken someone's life. My anger had been equally as strong. But having experienced this most destructive and debilitating emotion and finding a healthy outlet, I wanted to share it with these women.

This particular inmate slowly came around, and that sinister smirk turned to a half smile one night when she turned to me and said, "You know, I like your program. I could get into this. And I even like you—a little."

Other crippling emotions stalked many of the inmates. One emotion was depression—frozen rage. Its dark slime was deeply imbedded in the walls of this women's penitentiary. Like a serpent of despair, it slithered through cells, suffocating its victims and manifesting itself in the blank stare and the "prison shuffle."

Depression was an abstract ailment for me until I suffered my own after the rape. Like most people who are unacquainted with the malady first hand, I hadn't an inkling of the true contours of depression or the nature of the pain that many victims experience as the mind continues its insidious meltdown. Depression starts with a leaden and poisonous mood and develops into a deep melancholy, almost a mourning. Its victim becomes incapacitated. There is an emotional and physical distancing.

Inactivity—an abrupt halt to normal activity—is the hallmark of depression. Depression is anger turned inward; it is also the fifth stage of rape recovery, and probably the most dangerous one because most suicides occur during this stage. I know this because I came very close.

It was my first holiday season after moving back home. I was very despondent and I isolated myself from the world. Buttoning my heavy sweater, I stared at the winter wonderland outside my window. It was snowing again, soft flakes drifting out of the blackness lightening the night sky, but not my heart. Like a child, I pressed my nose against the window pane and then my palms and fingers spread-eagled as if I were about to jump through to the snow drifts below.

It was a very blue Christmas. I was obsessed with the snide stares and vicious voices of the gossips. With that problem came a terrifying fork in the road: Do I leave a promising career at a blue chip company or stay and endure the ceaseless stories and whispered glances? I felt like I was being raped again this time by the office witches. I overheard one call me "damaged goods."

Is this why I survived, God? Am I your damaged goods?

Dejected, I left the window and headed for my medicine cabinet. I collected the "pharmacy of pills" that I had been given. I lined them all up and then spread them out on the kitchen table. Together the multi-colored pills looked like a rainbow, and they were supposed to bring happiness and cure pain. But this pharmacy had failed me.

I went to the refrigerator and took out a container of plain nonfat yogurt; then I opened the drawer and removed a very large spoon and slowly proceeded to mash the rainbow of pills into the yogurt.

Suddenly, the absurdity of my actions hit me. You would think that if I intended to end my life I would at least do it with ice cream. Here I am counting calories before I draw my last breath. I'm health-conscious till the end. I threw my concoction down the toilet, totally disgusted with myself. *Okay, God, I'll stick around but I'm still not sure why.*

Well, now I know why I was spared, to help many of these depressed inmates. My healthy lifestyle and God saved me. But could I communicate this and inspire these poor souls whose future was so bleak?

The acrid torpor of prison is fertile ground for the vortex of pain and the downward spiral of the debilitating disease of depression. It would be a challenge, but having been there, I could empathize.

One girl stood out in our dance class because of her talent, enthusiasm, and angelic good looks. Long, curly, brown hair hung all the way down her back in artless, childish ripples that bounced merrily as she bopped to all the dance numbers. Pretty and petite, she would clasp her tiny hands with glee when I played her favorite song.

One time after class, she told me, "This isn't only the best thing that has happened to me in prison; this is the best thing that has happened to me in my life."

She was one of our regulars. And the night when a new group of women, who were very tough and insulting, came to class, she was our staunchest defender. She entreated the guards to forbid their attendance again. She begged us, "Please come back next week. Don't let tonight upset you."

Then, for no reason, she stopped coming to class. I asked her friends, "Where is Tamara tonight?"

They looked from one to the other and then to the floor, all the while fidgeting and shuffling their feet. "She's sick," one of the inmates said.

"She's sleeping," an inmate said when I asked the next week.

Finally, I heard, "She's depressed."

Each week, I would inquire about her. I asked her friends to let her know that I was looking for her and that I missed her. The third week, when they confessed about her depression, my words were measured but my message clear. "Tell Tamara that I understand. I, too, have been depressed. But I have a remedy that might work for her as it did for me. First, turn it over to God, for he cares, and second, keep busy and keep moving. Funny, that is what we do in this class. Please tell her that I care about her, and there is a hole in my front row and I need her to fill it."

Next week, my little friend was in her usual spot. I hugged her, and she took my hand. With luminous brown eyes, misty with emotion, she said, "I came back because you cared. No one ever cared before."

Sometimes, that's all it takes to dispel the cloud of depression.

But it's not that easy for most prisoners. A female inmate sees herself as a "loser" and feels it is "me against them." *Them* includes the police, courts, judges, lawyers, wardens, prison officers, chaplains, preachers, pastors, and churches. In most cases, there has been very little commitment to God or to a church. Even if a female inmate did have religious training in childhood, she now feels that God has let her down. Most assume that God and the church are for others.

Proudly, one of the inmates waved the photo in front of me. The summer before starting my aerobics class, she had weighed a hefty 275. Cocooned for years in a severely obese, dysfunctional body, she now was feeling good about herself and ready to shed the failures of the past, as well. Perhaps this rebirth put her in a confessionary mood. But I wasn't prepared for what she divulged. Guiltless and with complete candor, she announced, "I'm in here for child molesting." Seeing my look of shock, she added, "Oh, it's not as bad as it sounds. It was just with some neighborhood kids, and they exaggerated."

They warn you before you go into prison not to ask the inmates what they are in for. But most of the time, an inmate volunteers this information when you least expect it. I had just finished teaching a one-hour aerobic-dance class. I was perspiring profusely and frantically gathering my tapes before the guards locked the gym for the night when she decided to tell all.

The only response that I could muster was, "I'll keep you in my prayers." I did pray that night, and I asked God to give me wisdom in this situation. I could understand anger and depression on some level, but perversion of little children was something I couldn't stomach. Why she revealed this appalling information I will never know. I was an aerobic-dance instructor. I could encourage her about weight loss, but child molesting was out of my realm.

In retrospect, piecing together bits of information, I realized that she was desperately trying to be accepted for herself. She needed constant stroking in class. "I practiced the dance steps in my cell this week. Did you notice?"

I found out later that she had been abused as a child, a fact quite common among inmates, both male and female. It's a circular dance of perversion, abuse, and molestation, which continues on from generation to generation. A child who is abused often becomes an adult who abuses and so on and so on. Proven to be the source of a wide variety of criminal behavior, child abuse causes emotional wounds that often last into adulthood.

Child sexual abuse is an act of power, aggression, and violence imposed on a very vulnerable victim. The most common perpetrators of child sexual abuse are fathers, stepfathers, siblings, other family members, neighbors, or pedophiles. Pervasive Internet access has made it easier for sex offenders and serial pedophiles to prevail. Parental Internet supervision is essential.

If an act of abuse does occur, proper, ongoing therapy from a specialized professional is advised to prevent the inevitable downward spiral. The best that I could do for the inmate who was guilty of child molesting was to encourage her in her newfound self-esteem, to never judge her, and to try to love her.

Conversely, there were those instances when an inmate was wrongfully convicted of child molestation. "Look who is in our class," fumed one of my instructors. "I can't believe it. I read about her in the paper this morning. That's it; I quit. I will not help you teach a child abuser."

The woman in question had been convicted of molesting children in a day-care center that she ran with her brother and mother. The media were enticed by the titillating details and sex-abuse hysteria. Tried in the press, this woman and her family had been viewed as guilty before all the facts were in. Along with many other day-care providers, child sex abuse witch hunts had been set in motion by so-called child advocates and aggressive prosecutors, seeking attention from high-profile cases.

"Innocent until proven guilty," I retorted that night in our dance class. "We are here to teach aerobic dance, not to act as judge and jury."

Always an eager and pleasant student, the "abuser" approached the dances with enthusiasm and thanked us for coming every Thursday night. I was not surprised when several years later, she was proven innocent. A judge said new research showed that the prosecutors' suggestive and leading interview techniques had made it impossible to tell if the children, now teenagers, had been telling the truth. Stronger opinions stated that the children, coaxed by child therapists, had actually lied. The case was finally overturned, but not without damaging and permanently scarring the lives of three innocent people.

Justice was served, but this innocent woman lost more than eight years of her life.

This was also a lesson for all the Joy Dancers to never judge. We learned a lot about nonjudgmental love from a beautiful woman, the wife of a minister, who had a prison ministry for seven years. She summed up the responsibility of a prison volunteer. "They come to us half dead, abused, broken, angry, and bitter. Our job is to love them back to life." And love them she did! Through her actions, I saw the amazing power of love.

Before our dance outreach ever began, we went to a prison volleyball game to do some public relations for our aerobic-dance program. It was the prisoners versus these church volunteers, represented by this woman. When the game was over, the guard came in to round up the inmates. "Wait! I have to say a few words," this woman begged. "I just want you to know that the reason we come in here is because we love you."

I was watching the meanest, mannish-looking woman, a cap covering all semblance of a feminine coif. But suddenly, her face softened, and she said, "And we love you, too." Her voice trembled, and a tear stained her cheek. The power of love.

I also learned sensitivity from this woman. When I was preparing my dance numbers, I would say, "I have these great songs for my prisoners."

She would temper my enthusiasm and caution, "Susan, they're our 'ladies,' not our prisoners. They're human beings, and if we treat them kindly and with dignity, we'll reach them."

When I first talked to my pastor about my dance outreach, he told me that he thought that my testimony would be effective with these women. He said, "When I go into the prison, they scoff at me and tell me I don't know what it is like to be abused. And I don't. But you do. Go tell them your story. It will make an impression. You might be their wounded healer."

I didn't share my story before a large group in prison, but I did individually. Once, I received this response, "God must really love us a lot to send you in here. It's people like some of our brothers and fathers and boyfriends who rape and rob."

I always emphasized forgiveness when I talked with the inmates. And it was amazing to witness the healing power of forgiveness. When they felt forgiven and accepted, a burden was visibly lifted from their shoulders, and they expressed hope for the future. I also spoke about power over weaknesses. When I spoke about frailties, I included bad companions, food, alcohol, drugs, and any other addiction.

The average female inmate is under twenty-five years of age and comes from a broken home or a home where there is little love or discipline. She has nine years of schooling but actually only acquires a seventh-grade education. She has very little vocational training and has usually worked for minimum wage, if she has worked at all. These are just some of the reasons why a female inmate has such poor self-esteem and is terrified of trying to exist in a society that brands her a loser, a troublemaker, and an outcast.

The fastest growing sector of the prison population is women. Crimes perpetrated by women have increased 300 percent. The recidivism rate is very high among inmates. Eighty percent of crimes are committed by ex-offenders. Two out of three inmates are rearrested.

Sadly, I experienced this personally. One night, as I was leaving the prison, a former inmate and member of my class was coming in, handcuffed and held on each side by two male guards. When she saw me, she stared and then looked over her shoulder as she was led away—one last signal of desperation. I was shocked and speechless. She had only been out of prison for seven months.

I remembered the night she proudly announced to our class that her parole hearing was successful and that this would be her last dance class. We were so happy for her. We applauded and wished her well in her new life as a free woman. I urged some of the other inmates that she knew to invite her to come back to my class. She never showed up. I never found out what crime she committed to reenter prison. But the recidivism statistics came alive for me that night I saw her returned, shackled and scared.

One million children in the United States have a parent in prison. Eighty percent of female inmates are mothers. One of my students shared with me that both her parents, as well as her grandparents, had been in prison. She showed me a picture of her two-year-old son and said, "I need to break the cycle of crime. I don't want him to end up a felon. This has to stop with me."

Ninety-nine percent of the offenses committed by female inmates are drug related. Crimes such as passing bad checks, shoplifting, robbery, and prostitution are often committed to purchase drugs. Many of the women are also addicts, and they are recovering through treatment programs within the prison. I encouraged them in aerobics to hone their body to the nth degree—discipline it, control it, and master its weaknesses.

One woman's family had dubbed her the "golden girl" because she had won a beautiful-baby contest as an infant. She had dreams of becoming a model, but after having two children by age eighteen and a deadbeat husband, such a career was out of the question. Faced with the grim reality of raising her children alone, she turned to heroin to mask her fear and her fate. In a private nightmare of drugs, depression, and disastrous liaisons, her life spiraled ever downward. The once flawless model's body now had needle marks and bruises.

She told me about the night she was arrested. "I was cold," she said, "colder than I have ever been in my life. But I kept walking. I had to have it. The neighborhood was real seedy, and I shuddered when I thought of my two kids at home. I had left them in front of *Sesame Street* and a bowl of SpaghettiOs. I hoped I would be back before the program was over. I saw him in the distance, pacing nervously, looking from side to side. 'What took you so long?' he snapped. I reached into my jacket for the wad of bills I had removed from the cookie jar—this month's rent. The guy said, 'Did you tell anyone about this meeting place, 'cause—' It seemed that they came out of nowhere. Blue lights flashing, three cruisers. I was caught. A felon. My life would never be the same. I had hit rock bottom.

The dark side of the dream. My end. Heroin—that hell in a hypodermic—wracked my body to the core. Sometime during the horrors of withdrawal, I decided to turn my life around. I was gonna get it right this time. Learn something while I was in here. Go to school. Get a trade. I also wanted to get healthy. That's why I came to aerobics. Then I started thinking that I needed to get it right with God. I asked God to help me change. I have a job in here. I work with other inmates, and sometimes, they complain about the work. I remembered what you said about going the extra mile, and I ask if I can help them. You know, I'm gonna make it this time because I'm okay in here." She smiled and pointed to her heart.

I was told by the chaplain that many of the prison's most troubled inmates had joined our aerobic-dance class and that she had seen them change. She said she encouraged their participation. I made a tape of our class so that they could get together more often during the week to practice on their own.

"Hey, I couldn't help noticing that you are really bulking up," I said to one of my best dancers who stood directly behind me every week. "You don't want to get too heavy because you won't move as well, and I depend on you to help the other girls when you practice."

"You know I love to dance, and I love your class," she said, "but I'm bulking up so that no one will ever hurt me again. I have a T-shirt, too." She turned around to show me what it read, "Say no to violence against women." Then she said, "We had a walkathon here for those of us who have experienced domestic abuse, and we got these shirts. There is a group of us, and we stick together."

Though most of the crimes committed by women are nonviolent, some are in prison for murder. Most are long-term victims of domestic abuse, who daily tread the brink of destruction. Some kill their spouse or boyfriend in self-defense. One-third of all adult female murder victims are murdered by a husband or a boy-friend.[1]

I became more sensitized to this issue after I saw the T-shirt and noticed the others wearing it. One night, a woman opened the door of the gym and peeked in at my class before entering. She stood awkwardly in back and slowly advanced, but her steps were half hearted—a forced shuffle. As she came closer, I noticed a prominent scar that stretched across her forehead and ran down her right cheek, severely disfiguring her face. Her eyes were dulled by sadness so oppressive and palpable that I felt my own shoulders drooping. She was wearing the T-shirt.

I forced myself to approach her, shake her hand, and welcome her to class. She came every week after that, and I learned her story. Her name was Diane, and after years of savage, physical abuse, she had shot her husband. She didn't seem to be as concerned with her disfigured face as I was, but it was her husband's last act of butchery before he died.

She had stayed with him because she had four children and no income. She also didn't believe in divorce. As a little girl, she was enthralled with TV family sitcoms, dreaming of the day when she would be the perfect wife and mother. "I just wanted to be Donna Reed," she said. "My own childhood was difficult, so I vowed that I would have my own perfect family. I've heard it said that you marry someone like your parents. Well, I married someone even worse. My life is over. I've lost my kids. My only comfort is the women in here who have suffered the same fate."

One fifth to one half of the world's female population will become victims of domestic violence. Like Diane, many remain in the home for economic reasons until one day, they can't take it anymore, and they kill the abuser.

But in the eyes of the law, it is still murder. Despite overwhelming evidence of sadistic physical abuse, many of these women, including Diane, spend years in prison, despite appeals. To protect women and their children who suffer abuse, there are safe houses, shelters, and counselors, but not enough to stem the tide of domestic violence. The statistics don't include the countless women who suffer emotional and verbal abuse, including threats, blackmail, and the belittling of worth, talents, opinions, friends, looks, or spiritual affiliation. It can last for years and never get physical, or it can escalate into slapping, hitting, black eyes, punching, and even murder.

From the opulent suburbs to the poorest ghettos, it is America's most heinous secret that behind the doors of many homes, sit abused women, some plotting escape, others stoically staying and trying to mend the situation. It is a problem that is ongoing with no end in sight. Diane is still in prison despite countless appeals. Injustice has a face, and it is disfigured.

Peering through a prism of pain came Patricia. She entered my class wearing the T-shirt as well as bruises like ink stains, open sores, and gashes; one long, protruding vein resembled a ribbon of dried blood. No one had ever come to an aerobic-dance class in that condition. They had come in pregnant, sometimes very pregnant, and in every emotional state, from anger to depression, but none with physical and mental wounds as raw as Patricia's.

"Do you have a medical clearance?" I asked.

"Yeah, she's cool. She doesn't need a clearance," said one of my regulars.

As soon as I reached her, a large legion of the "T-shirt" group surrounded her protectively. "I told you we stick together," said my best dancer. "She's one of us, and she needs to be with us."

"Please, can I stay?" pleaded Patricia. "I want to take your class, but maybe tonight, I could just watch."

"Sure," I relented.

"One more thing," she added. "I heard that sometimes you pray with … with tormented people to comfort them. After class, could you do that with me?"

"Okay," I quivered, my heart aching for her. I didn't know how I could teach after seeing this anguished woman, but somehow, I got through it.

I learned her haunting story. She had lived for years with a bipolar husband, who frequently went off his medication or diffused its purpose with massive amounts of alcohol. They had two beautiful children, a girl aged seven and a boy aged four. Patricia lived for her kids, and that was why she had stayed with this man.

But one night, his violent rages exploded like a volcano. She had no idea what had set him off. She tried to focus and walk to another area of the house until his anger subsided. As she lengthened her stride, she felt two strong hands turn her around. His face was inches from hers, a huge face, with wild eyes, a jagged vein throbbing in his forehead, yellow teeth bared, nostrils flared in defiance. His hands moved from her shoulders to her throat, and he shook Patricia the way a mongrel dog shakes a dead mouse.

She couldn't breathe. She was choking, spitting. She felt like she would vomit.

"You ruined my life, and now, I've ruined yours. I killed our two kids, your two loves, and now, I'm going to kill you."

The moment he mentioned her children, Patricia summoned superhuman strength like a one-hundred-pound woman who can lift a truck and pushed him away, running for the kitchen. She grabbed the biggest carving knife she could find, and the next time he came at her, she was ready for him. She stabbed him once through the heart, which killed him.

But the worst was yet to come. Frantically, she ran from room to room, searching for her children, calling out their names. She found them in a trash heap in back of her house, lying side-by-side, arms curled as if reaching for one another. "You're nothing but rubbish," was the phrase he had often spat at the kids. Now, he had seen to it that they were.

Patricia fell to her knees, gashing her leg, knife still in hand. Loud, inhuman sobs of anguish emanated from her. Neighbors came running when they heard the strange sobs that sounded like a tortured, wild animal. One called 9-1-1. When the police arrived, Patricia still had the knife in her hand. The police handcuffed her, accusing her of the slayings.

Patricia is still in prison. All her appeals have been denied.

Meredith had talent and presence, eyes sparkling, lips wet red, and a body transformed by a few simple turns and torso moves into a tiny, twirling magnum opus. Though streetwise, she was still an urchin underneath. An electric hussy with a maverick style, she possessed a unique and commanding beauty. She was playful and unabashedly flirtatious with a tawny plumage of golden brown hair that looked amber in sunlight, chestnut at twilight. She handled herself with the discipline and confidence of a bareback rider in the circus, who makes the most difficult trick look easy. She was impetuous. She dazzled. She was a showstopper. You could always spot one.

"You move really well," I gushed.

"I never thought that I would be in an aerobic-dance class," Meredith said. "But I do have experience, sort of. I was a stripper in a downtown nightclub. They pulled me in for that and prostitution."

"Well, if you want to become a legitimate, professional dancer or choreographer," I said, "I could help you. I really believe you could make it if you set your mind to it."

"That's my dream," Meredith said, her voice trembling with emotion.

"Well," I said, "let's see if you can choreograph a song for the class. This is how you write it out." I pulled out a notebook and showed her how to pair the moves with the beats of the song on paper. "You can finish it this week and show me your creation next week. I can bring you a reading list of all the great choreographers. And I can recommend many dance teachers and schools when you get out."

In my prison classes, they came from quiet working-class towns, from inner-city war zones, from pricey suburban cul-de-sacs, and from every class of society. But there was one who came from the other side of the globe.

From the killing fields of Cambodia—that terrain of terror—came a Buddhist nun. In the blackness of night, this fragile figure became one of the boat people, fleeing the Khmer Rouge for the United States. A trip of torment ensued, but despite overcrowding, uncharted waters, and monsoon rains, she somehow made it to America's shores.

In a poor, run-down neighborhood, she happily began a new life, eager to work at minimum wage, so grateful for her first taste of freedom. Walking home one evening after working overtime, she was jumped by five men, beaten, knifed, and gang-raped with unbridled cruelty. Later, in a moment of rage, she retaliated by trying to shoot the gang leader. She was caught and sent to prison. Six weeks later, she discovered she was pregnant. The child was born in prison and taken from her after one month. Abandoned and depressed, she looked into the darkest corners of her experience and into the dancing demons of despair and knew what she had to do. "I hoisted myself up to a self-made rope and looped it around my neck. With trembling hands, I tightened the noose. I took two steps forward and started to jump from the chair. Then my baby's face flashed in front of me. Choking, I decided I couldn't go through with it. But I needed help. I mouthed the words, but nothing came out. I tried to scream, but my voice betrayed me. I screamed and screamed. But it was a silent scream."

Help did arrive, and she was hospitalized. She refused aid from doctors, prison officials, and even the chaplain. She told them that there was only person with whom she would speak—me. Night after night, she cried out to me, saying, "My family has disowned me, and I am now a ruined woman."

I would remind her of my story, promising that she, too, would heal. I also encouraged her to reveal her feelings because that, too, would be the beginning of healing. I added, "There are depths of your pain that I can't begin to understand, but I can at least be here to comfort you. I know this sounds impossible, but someday, I believe you will forgive these men, and you will then move on with your life."

It was a divine tableau. Only God could bring together a blond from Boston and a Cambodian refugee who had served in Buddha's temple. To silence her anguished voice, I reached out an arm of love and caring.

Day by day, she healed. She looked forward to the day when she would be reunited with her three children, including the child from the rape.

10

Wounded Healer in a Dance Symphony

"It's Halloween next week. Don't show up. We throw a party for them on Halloween. You're not invited."

And so, the Joy Dancers were unceremoniously dismissed from next week's class. We understood though it might have been communicated while we were in class with the inmates and with a modicum of civility. So I was really surprised to receive a call at work Halloween afternoon, insisting that I drop by the prison to pick up some paperwork. Orders and demands had never been big with me, so I was rather annoyed at this command performance.

It was spooky walking to the entrance without my dance troupe. But I made it to the front window and told them why I was there. The female guard nodded knowingly, handed me a manila folder, and then gave me an eerie warning, "Don't open this until you get home."

I felt chills traveling down my spine, but after all, it was Halloween.

Safely ensconced in my home, I plopped down on my couch, expecting the worst. I opened the folder and saw a small envelope addressed to "Joy Dancers, Thursday Volunteers." When I opened the envelope, I saw a beautiful card, which read, "A day is made more beautiful when touched with kindness. Thank you for your special thoughtfulness." It was signed by all the inmates with their individual greetings. Some of the sentiments were "We just wanted to let you know how special you volunteers are to us. Please keep coming. We didn't want the Halloween party; we wanted to dance. Thanks for caring about us."

I cried like a baby. For all the bureaucracy, to touch even one broken person, to provide a hopeful perspective to the darkest life made all the aggravation worth it.

And the prison's rules and regulations did get more Draconian each year. The biggest change that hurt us was the new entrance. Though far less ominous-looking than the original one, this entrance forced us to go through more checkpoints, more searches, more signings, and more waiting. Worst of all, it was quite a distance from the prison gym. No matter how early we got there, we were always late for class.

Drenching rain added to bureaucracy one night. Each checkpoint seemed longer and nastier as if they were trying to discourage us from ever coming back. Also, that night, they decided to have us cut through the prison yard. While pelting rain ravaged us, I slipped, and my shoes and legs were covered in mud. By the time we arrived at the gym, we were an hour late, but the girls were still there.

They were totally disgusted when they saw my muddy appearance. "Susan, how can you teach us when you are covered in mud," they complained.

"This is how," I said while removing my muddy shoes and socks. "And tonight, I will also teach a new dance; how about a little 'Respect' by Aretha Franklin. Lord knows I could use a little tonight."

"Cool. Aretha's my favorite," said one of the inmates. "Let's go."

I love a challenge. And the girls loved the new dance number. I wasn't about to let bureaucracy undue the strides I had made with the inmates. In addition to the increased bureaucracy, I also noticed a decline in the behavior of prison personnel.

One night, we were performing one of our routines. I was in my usual spot with my back to the inmates so that they could follow my choreography. I looked over my shoulder to see how they were doing, and they had stopped moving. "What's going on?" I asked. "When you stop, you lose the aerobic benefit; you stop burning fat." One of my regulars motioned me to the side of the gym. "Okay, two-minute water break," I said.

"Have you seen that guard who keeps peeping through the door?" the inmate asked me.

At that moment, the door opened slightly, and a four-eyed, large, male guard was peering inside at all the female inmates. "He has the keys to all our rooms," another inmate said. "At night, he comes in and stands over us while we're sleeping. Maybe we can't control that, but we won't dance if he watches."

I asked, "Have you complained to his superiors about his coming into your rooms?"

"Sure. Lots of times," the inmate said. "But he just makes something up, and they believe him over us."

"We've all complained," said the first inmate, "but no one listens or cares." Some of the other girls had joined us.

"Class is almost over," I said. "Please, just humor me and keep dancing for the last number. I'm just a lowly volunteer, but I promise I'll think and pray about this and do whatever I can. Now, everyone back to the dance floor. Okay, one last time from the top."

God, this is appalling. What should I do? A volunteer is just one step above an inmate in the prison caste system. If I speak up, they could throw me out over a leering lothario. Just what this place needs: a big Brutus in a cauldron of chaos.

Even though I didn't look, I knew the pervert was stealing glances. I willed myself to stay in my spot. I visualized my dancing feet glued to the floor. Feisty Susan had replaced fearful Susan. The two had fought for center stage ever since the rape. I preferred feisty Susan, and tonight, feisty was queen, but I had the good sense to rein her in—for now, anyway.

The last dance ended. I bid good night by giving each girl a pat on the back. I collected all my tapes and donned my parka. I lagged behind my troupe and the female escort guard. I was still disturbed by the disgusting story. As I left the gym, there he was in front of me. I saw him put his hand on the backside of a small blond girl. Feisty became furious, but I still had to be cautious. "Hey, guys," I called, "I left something in the gym. I'll catch up to you."

"Make it snappy!" yelled the escort guard without turning her head.

I quickly jumped in front of the sleazy guard and cornered him. "I saw what you did to that girl," I said. "And I saw you opening the door to my class to get your jollies leering at my dancers. I heard you also go into their rooms at night and stare at them while they're sleeping. If you ever bother any of these girls again, I'll not only get you fired, but I'll see to it that you make the front page of the newspaper."

All this time, the guard was backing up against the wall, terrified of little ol' me. He was a great, big bully, who backed down when confronted by a woman half his size. I ran to catch up to my group, who were oblivious to my encounter. I never saw that bully guard again. He never showed up at my class, nor did the girls ever complain of any more nightly visits. He also didn't report me to the authorities.

I must admit I felt more than a bit of self-satisfaction. I felt triumphant. I had progressed from the mute, pitiful rape victim of the lineups to a confrontational advocate for the rights of the powerless, and no one had less power than a female inmate. If they couldn't have power, they could, at least, have self-worth. But I learned that before you could make any progress with prisoners, you had to be able to look them in the eye and say "I believe in you" and mean it.

I noticed a change when the girls saw that we believed in them. Some of them tried so hard to please us: practicing during the week, thanking us profusely, and beaming when they heard compliments on their dancing, such as, "Good job! Great technique! Looking good!"

If I had owned my own health club or dance studio, I would have said to many of them, "When you get out, I'd like to train you to be an instructor in my club."

I felt that if they knew that someone believed in them and if they were doing something that they liked, they would handle the responsibility and stay straight. I believed that people could change when someone believed in them—and gave them a chance.

I hadn't always believed this. For a long while after the rape, I strongly advocated the death penalty. I thought that heinous crimes such as rape should be punishable by death. In fact, during my anger phase, I used to make the statement that I would actually pull the lever on the electric chair to rid society of these sadistic criminals.

Well-meaning friends would back me up and say that the Old Testament talked about the wrath of God against evildoers and that God was only against murder without just cause. But I had a Sunday-school teacher who pointed to the same Old Testament, cited Noah and the flood, and reminded us that God said he would never destroy humanity in this way again. This teacher interpreted this as a plea against taking a life for any reason.

My change of mind was based not only on this Sunday-school teacher but on my experiences with the prisoners. When we came into prison as the Joy Dancers, we gave them a rope to grab onto, a chance for fun and fellowship, and, with the music and the movement, the chance to dance. I saw the cynical faces that entered class every week and the faces that left. I saw joy on those faces.

I once read a fairytale about twin brothers. As they got older, one of the boys left home and involved himself in debauchery and evil living. He met a magician, who turned him into a wolf because of his sins. Years later, the other brother was walking through the woods and was attacked by his brother, the wolf. Rather than defend himself, the brother simply looked with compassion and great love at the ferocious wolf. And as he did, the wolf features became human again, and his brother was restored.

The power of love can change anyone.

After the rape, I had only two choices: hate or love. I could either hate the men who had assaulted me and others of their ilk, both male and female, or I could learn to love them.

I chose love.

I had been on both sides—from the cruel stories of man's inhumanity to man, resonating through the lineups, to the softening of a hardened convict who had encountered kindness and love. My commitment was to bring these two worlds together because I had a unique experience in both. In my own small way, I saw myself bridging the gap. And because I had known the nightmare, I could foster the dream. Now, nearly eight years later, everything that I believe and everything that I have become is because of the rape. My life cannot be separated from it. I have heard individuals speak about their adversity and say, "Despite the pain and suffering, I would never trade this experience for anything."

Would I?

I have to be honest as I have tried to be throughout this book. I shudder to think of going through the rape experience again. It hurt mentally and physically. Recovery took many years, and I still have residual physical problems. A result of the abuse I suffered is severe TMJ, which is a condition where the jaw locks up. When my TMJ flares up, I suffer from blinding, viselike headaches and an aching jaw, cheekbones, and skull. Most medical opinions render TMJ (especially if caused by trauma) a severe disorder, resulting in searing, agonizing, and incapacitating pain. I also have tinnitus, a ringing in my ears that often accompanies TMJ. Every time a TMJ episode occurs, I am reminded of the brutality of that night.

And yet, despite the enormity of the pain, I cannot say I would want to go back to being the person I was.

I was showing an older and wiser friend of mine two photos: one of me before the rape and one after. He made an interesting observation. "The picture of you before the rape is quite lovely," my friend observed. "Your skin is smooth. No wrinkles. You are unsmiling but determined. Your eyes are direct and focused. Unflinching. Cold. The other picture has many battle scars. It shows the toll that suffering has taken. But the smile is warm. And look at those eyes! There is love in those eyes."

Pain and suffering bring us to a fork in the road. It is not possible to remain unchanged. You can let the anger and bitterness eat away at you, or you can let it transform you.

It has been said that adversity introduces a person to her true self. I like the new woman I met. Underneath the superficial facade of the shallow dancer I used to be was someone genuine, someone strong, someone caring—a woman of compassion.

When I first began the prison outreach, I wanted to be an example. I wanted to encourage inmates about physical fitness, but I also wanted to keep my distance. But something happened as the weeks wore on. I really started to care about each girl as an individual—precious in God's sight with the potential to do great things.

After I was raped, I couldn't have children. Never would I know my own baby's cry, the feel of my fuzzy-haired infant cradled in my arms, a chorus of contagious coos and squeals, or that special intimacy known only to mother and child. For years, I shed bitter tears, wondering how God could allow this additional suffering. Then, one night in prayer, it came to me.

The inmates are your children. They want to please you. They need someone to believe in them. And you have a mother's love. Go and give it to them. Give it to your ladies.

Maybe that is why I cared so much. I'm not claiming in any way that my prison outreach was a perfect panacea because the allure of the old life and the old ways was tempting. Inmates went back to the same neighborhoods and the same friends and often returned to the same habits. No volunteer group has yet found the ideal antidote for recidivism.

But for those who wanted to embrace a blueprint for a healthy lifestyle and experience joining a dance troupe led by moral, ethical teachers who cared deeply about their welfare, I offered the Joy Dancers. And if I could prevent it by words, deeds, and fervent prayers, they would, at least, think twice before they committed another crime.

It has been said that God is present among suffering people. I truly felt that he was there among these broken, troubled women. Much has been cynically written about jailhouse conversions, but I saw those sincere and repentant souls, and they were earnest in their decision.

I also believe that God blesses those who reach out to hurting people. To paraphrase a line from the movie *Chariots of Fire*, "When I dance, I can feel his pleasure." I passed on that pleasure and tried to break through an arc of misery.

I guess this elation was not only evident in my feet but on my face, as well. Friends told me that I glowed when I spoke about the dance outreach, and people picked this up, especially the inmates. I wanted the girls to feel the same joy and sense of self-worth when they successfully executed routines.

To raise their self-esteem, I decided to have a Christmas recital where the prisoners would perform all their dance numbers in red Joy Dancers T-shirts, their gifts to keep. I wanted to give them one special moment in time, a night to remember. I wanted them to experience the spotlight where they would take center stage. The audience would be comprised of their families and friends, other prisoners, and members of my church.

Rehearsals were intense. The inmates took it very seriously. To my surprise, they wanted to know the correct name and pronunciation of every dance step either from me or their classmates. I overheard two girls talking, and one girl said, "I asked you whether we're doing a chassé or a pas de bourrée."

I smiled, thinking how far they had come. I had a sudden inspiration—a plan to make each girl a singular sensation.

"Listen up, ladies. You will all have a chance to perform a short solo. You've all heard the Whitney Houston song 'One Moment In Time.'[1] There is a section in that song that will allow each of you to demonstrate your favorite move. It can be a step you learned in class or one of your own creations. I will need to see it first, so have it ready for next week. I will choreograph the rest of the song around your solos."

The excitement was palpable, and the buzz rose to crescendo level. "We're going to be stars," I heard one woman say.

"Wait till you see my solo," said another woman.

The first woman spoke up again, saying, "Girl, once I do mine, you can all hang it up."

"Hey, teach," said the second woman, "do you think there will be any talent scouts in the audience?"

I rolled my eyes at that one, but I was glad that they were enjoying themselves and happy that I came up with the idea. The recital definitely bonded them and made them forget their dreary surroundings for a while. And dancing a solo gave them something to shoot for, a performance goal.

Just when I thought everything was going well, someone tapped me on the shoulder. "Do you plan to teach the steps tonight?" It was Lucy.

"What steps, Lucy?"

"The steps to all the dances."

My jaw dropped, and my instructors looked shocked. "But we've been learning them all year," I said. "If you were having trouble, why didn't you ask one of us for help?"

"I was ashamed," lamented Lucy. "I always stayed in back so no one would see me."

I took a deep breath. "Okay, I promise one of us will work with you so that you will have all the steps down perfectly."

"I also want to talk to you about my solo," Lucy continued. "I want to jump high in the air. When I was a little girl, the kids would laugh at me when I couldn't jump because I was so fat. If I could just jump for my solo, I would be so happy."

"Okay," I said, "show me how you jump."

Lucy was very heavyset, and dance and aerobic movements did not come easy. She had been in my class for two years. "I can't do it, yet, but you said in class that with God, all things are possible. So I pray every night."

I knew I had to come up with something fast. "We could do some really pretty moves with your arms, Lucy," I said.

"No, I want to jump," Lucy insisted. "I need to jump. And you said—"

"I know," I broke in. "Let's go to that space over there and see what we can come up with."

As I followed her, I turned once to look at my instructors, who were mouthing the words "You said" and snickering. This would be a challenge.

The rest of the recital program was shaping up nicely. Though it didn't have the sizzling choreography of a Broadway musical, it marked the debut of my chorus line of convicts. The blood, sweat, and tears they poured into it equaled that of any professional dancer. I was amazed at their passion, dedication, and drive.

"No matter what happens at the recital," I said, "I want you to know that I am so proud of each of you. You have worked hard, you've helped one another, and you've spread your enthusiasm throughout the prison. Congratulate yourselves. You have a sold-out premiere. This gym will be jam-packed. Give yourselves a round of applause."

Whistles, catcalls, jumping up and down, screams, and thunderous applause ensued.

"Well, that was boisterous," I said, laughing. "Now, I want to teach you how to bow theatrically so you will be ready for your standing ovation." I demonstrated the bow as they watched solemnly. "After you have finished performing," I said, "you will hear the sound of applause. It will feel as if a thousand arms are embracing you. And you will feel warm and cherished inside. Remember that feeling, tuck it inside your heart, and retrieve it on down days because one afternoon for two hours, a huge audience was so crazy about you that they clapped and cheered. They thought you were special."

Recital day came. We had it on a Saturday afternoon. The audience members from my church arrived by chartered bus. Relatives of the inmates filled the waiting room, and the other prisoners who wanted to view this spectacle lined up outside the gym.

The girls were busy fixing each other's hair and reviewing the dance steps. A group of their fellow inmates, who didn't dance but were great with tools, designed a maroon, velvet curtain that would open and close as they pulled the ropes—just like a real theater curtain. I recruited one to pull the curtain and another to handle the recorder.

The attendees were all patted down, put in the holding room, and escorted to the gym. Then the inmate attendees were checked and let in one by one, taking the last three rows.

Backstage with my nervous group, I suggested that we all join hands, and I asked that they close their eyes, take a deep breath, and listen. I told them that I found this poem in a book, untitled and anonymous, and I recited it to them. I dubbed it "The Dancer's Prayer":

> Giver of life, Creator of all that is lovely,
> Teach me to sing the words to your song;
> I want to feel the music of living
> And not fear the sad songs,
> But from them make new songs
> Composed of both laughter and tears.
> Teach me to dance to the sounds of your world and your people,
> I want to move in rhythm with your plan;
> Help me to try to follow your leading,
> To risk even falling,
> To rise and keep trying
> Because you are leading the dance.

A few of the girls wiped away a tear. "Now, go out there and make me proud. Break a leg!" They looked at me in horror. I chuckled. "That's a stage expression. It means 'good luck.' Let me give a brief introduction to the audience before we raise the curtain."

I addressed the audience. "Good afternoon. Welcome to the first annual recital of the Joy Dancers. We are a volunteer dance troupe that meets every Thursday night for fun, fitness, and fellowship. We also learn new dance routines, choreographed numbers with an aerobic spin for exercise. Oh, by the way, I'm Susan or, as the girls refer to me, 'the teach.' They have worked so hard to present a program that you will thoroughly enjoy. Without any further ado, I give you the Joy Dancers."

The curtain rose. We were poised. An expectant hush fell over the audience. I cued the inmate assigned to the recorder. "Hit it."

We began our well-rehearsed routines. The audience cheered and clapped, and the prison chaplain actually got up for one number and danced with the inmates.

Then it was time for their solos. We danced together to the beginning of the piece, and then I stepped aside, the girls aligned single file, and I signaled the first soloist.

"Give me one moment in time, when I'm more than I thought I could be."[2] Whitney belted out her song as each inmate lived it.

The audience rose to their feet for all the solos, applauding vigorously.

I held my breath as Lucy approached. *Please, God, let her jump.* She did it! Triumphant tears followed her solo. Gone forever was her cruel title as "the fat girl who couldn't even jump." Though I wouldn't sign her up immediately for pole vaulting or the long jump, my heart told me there were other victories ahead.

At the very end when the girls bowed, they received a standing ovation. Their faces were beaming; some had tears in their eyes. They had experienced the spotlight; they had their moment in time. Arms embraced them. They felt cherished.

In the swirl of bodies, both audience and dancers, a flurry of emotions fused: tears and tender embraces, words of praise and prideful smiles, kudos and compliments from cellmates. One prison official called it, "an intriguing wonder."

Punch and cookies followed our aerobic-dance recital as relatives hugged their dancers; many of the inmates in the audience talked to me about signing up; my church members spoke to the chaplain about the success of the program.

The prison chaplain revealed her secret to my church group. She had peeked through the door almost every week to learn the steps to her favorite song. She had also monitored the prison's most problematic inmates, who had taken my class. "They were so docile in dance class, concentrating on new routines," the chaplain said. "Hard to believe that an hour before they had initiated a food fight in the cafeteria."

And one of the inmates from my class told them, "Susan released us, not only from our self-imposed prisons, but for an hour a week from this prison. She made us feel free. There was no part of us pent up, unexpressed. She carried us through the music, the rhythms, and the dance routines. Today, we celebrate every step for what it is—a miracle, an accomplishment."

I looked around at all the smiling faces as they seamlessly mingled—worlds of vivid contrasts and fluent extremes together in harmony. I wished it could be that way for more than a couple of hours. But the attendees would soon leave, the girls would go back to their cells, and today would just be a memory.

But for me, a part of my identity would forever be carved in the crumbling walls of this poisoned place, this gulag of grief, this archipelago of remorse. Because I was able to crack the misery code and convicts became dancers, and fantasy replaced reality, if only for a moment. An eternal instant.

Ever since that recital, I've had this recurring dream. The dream is that when I die and I meet my God, he will say to me, "There are some people here waiting for you. It's real easy to pick them out, because they all arrived in costume."

And from every side they will come, in shirts as colorful as their lives were on earth. And those whom the world called trash, he will call trophies. Quickly, we will assemble in a chorus line. I'll take my place among them—their wounded healer. And we will perform a dance symphony.

His eyes will dance as we dance, and he will smile on a prison program founded in his name. And as we finish, very slowly but very deliberately, he will lift two large hands, and he will applaud.

Notes

Preface

1. The Rape, Abuse & Incest National Network (RAINN) calculation based on United States Department of Justice National Crime Victimization Survey Data, 2005.

Epigraph

Calvin Miller, *The Singer* (Downer's Grove, IL: InterVarsity Press, 1975), 143.

Chapter 4 The Dancer Returns

1. Corrie ten Boom, *Each New Day* (Old Tappan, NJ: Revell, 1977), 109.

2. Michael Sembello, "Maniac," *Bossa Nova Hotel* CD Release Gold Album, 1983.

Chapter 5 The Dance of Anger

1. Michael Sembello, "Maniac," *Bossa Nova Hotel* CD Release Gold Album, 1983.

2. Michael Sembello, "Maniac," *Bossa Nova Hotel* CD Release Gold Album, 1983.

Chapter 6 Forgiveness: The Signature Piece

1. Charles Swindoll, *Improving Your Serve* (Waco, TX: Word, 1981).

Chapter 7 New Steps for a New Life

1. The Dance Notebook Journal (Philadelphia: Running Press, 1984).

2. Based on a speech given by Tom Sullivan at the "Celebrate 1983" Million Dollar Roundtable, Dallas, Texas.

3. Corrie ten Boom, *The Hiding Place* (Old Tappan, NJ: Revell, 1961).

Chapter 9 Tales of the Dance

1. Bureau of Justice Statistics, Crime Data Brief, Intimate Partner Violence, February, 2003.

Chapter 10 Wounded Healer in a Dance Symphony

1. Whitney Houston, "One Moment In Time," *The Greatest Hits* (2000), Arista Records, Inc.

2. Whitney Houston, "One Moment In Time," *The Greatest Hits* (2000), Arista Records, Inc.

About the Author
Susan Lee-Titus

Susan Lee-Titus is an author, speaker, dancer, and communications and media specialist. She also teaches aerobics and is a member of the drama group Act One.

Ms. Lee-Titus's diversified background includes serving as a local talk-show host, cable news anchor, drama critic, and host of *That's Entertainment!*—a weekly culture and arts program. Prior to that, she taught drama, speech, and communications at various colleges and universities in the New England area.

She attended Emerson College, where she earned her masters degree in communications, graduating with honors.

Ms. Lee-Titus is the founder of the Joy Dancers, a prison outreach program that teaches aerobic dance to female inmates as an outlet for anger and stress.

The author of *The Dancer: One Woman's Journey from Tragedy to Triumph*, Susan Lee-Titus's writing is also featured in the anthology *Setting the Captives Free*.

As a rape victim, Ms. Lee-Titus sheds new light on this brutal act and also lays the foundation for hope and forgiveness in *The Dancer Returns: From Victim to Victory*. She resides in a suburb of Washington, D.C.

978-0-595-42414-6
0-595-42414-7

Printed in the United States
88128LV00002B/25-42/A